The Forward Prizes for Poetry are supported by Forward Worldwide,
a leading content marketing agency based in London and Shanghai.
Forward Worldwide creates beautifully crafted, highly targeted
customer communications for clients such as Patek Philippe, Tesco,
Standard Life, Luštica Bay, American Express and Barclays.
Forward's bespoke magazines, websites, ezines and emails are
produced in 38 languages and reach customers in 172 countries.
For more information, please visit www.forwardww.com

The Forward book of poetry
2014

The Forward book of poetry
2014

FORWARD

LONDON

First published in Great Britain by
Forward Worldwide · The Griffin Building · 83 Clerkenwell Road
London EC1R 5AR
in association with
Faber and Faber · Bloomsbury House · 74-77 Great Russell Street
London WC1B 3DA

ISBN 978 0 571 30497 4 (paperback)

Printed and bound in the UK by CPI Group (UK) Ltd, Croydon CR0 4YY

A CIP catalogue reference for this book
is available at the British Library.

To Susannah Herbert

Contents

Highly Commended Poems 2013

Foreword

POETRY IS THE BOMB and the safe exploding of the bomb.

If this sounds too violent an image, consider this: modern life is in a state of siege. We know that the world is run by the rich for the rich and it appears that there is nothing we can do about it. Our common wealth has been destroyed by greed. Our planet is being destroyed by greed and desperation. The poor are poorer.

In the West we are bombarded by advertising and spin, exhausted by the juggle of work and family, we try to sleep under nightly air-raids of anxiety. Depression is the new disease.

Elsewhere in the world, Fundamentalism seeks a return to medieval values with modern weapons.

Everywhere in the world, burka or six-inch heels, anorectic or cosmetic, women are under siege in their own bodies.

What has poetry to say?

The poem as the bomb is the poem as the flash of energy capable of blasting an opening into our private bunker. Whether we are huddled away trying not to notice how bad things are, or giving up, or feeling that no-one will ever rescue us, the poem lets in air and light. The poem can do this by changing the images in our head – the endless replay of the same movie where our lives get stuck. The poem can do this by replacing the worn-out language of TV and politics, the karate-chop soundbites of daily news, with words that say something real.

We live with an increasing sense of unreality. The poem is real.

Try this: stand in front of the mirror and read or recite a poem you love and watch the change in your face. Feel the change in your body. The pulse and breath of the poem is affecting. When I was having a nervous breakdown the only thing that could silence the crazy voices in my head was the stronger voice of the poem – first blasting through the chaos, then working to contain the chaos, until my own voice, and silence, could be heard again.

When poetry has done its work as the bomb, it can then contain our sorrow and sadness, our anger and violence. The poem is not afraid of feeling, any feeling, all feeling, and the poem gives us back the words we need so that we can say how we feel. When we have no language we are not fully human. Mass culture dilutes the strength of language, dosing it with soap opera cliché and bad lines from celebrity self-help.

Poetry is not convoluted or remote, not arcane or deliberately difficult. Coleridge called a poem 'the best words in the best order.' Poetry is a practical art. You can rely on it. It will not break under your weight.

We made our choices looking for poems that used a lit-up living language and had a sense of purpose. We decided to break the rules and include six books, not five, in Best First Collection because five would have been arbitrary, whereas six allowed us to show the range and strength of the work being done now by new writers.

Best Collection was difficult. This is a powerful year for poetry. But poetry is not one thing – readers will recognise the obvious excellence of established poets like Michael Symmons Roberts and Glyn Maxwell, but we were all moved by Rebecca Goss's raw, unfinished, still-drying handprints, as she struggled to find a language for loss at its most painful – the death of a child.

Best Single Poem and Highly Commended will give pleasure and debate in equal measure, as they did for all of us doing the judging. We have all had to give up favourites, but this year's choices are a genuine showcase of the scope and depth of poetry now.

Everything in life is propositional. The way we live is not a law, like gravity. Poetry is a private act with a public responsibility. We are better for the poem. The intervention of the poem, reader by reader, one by one, equips us for the larger interventions necessary and brave, against the illusion that nothing can change.

Jeanette Winterson, *June 2013*

Preface

'To HAVE GREAT POETS, there must be great audiences too.' Walt Whitman made this claim at the dawn of mass literacy, in nineteenth-century America.

I founded the Forward Prizes for Poetry – which sift through the year's crop of poetry to arrive at the contents of this annual anthology – some 22 years ago because I wanted to find Whitman's great audiences, the people who would respond strongly to poetry if only they could find their way through the poetry maze.

They had to exist, because I'd heard such audiences talk with informed passion about contemporary music, fiction, design, films, sculpture, buildings. Contemporary poetry, however, didn't seem to strike quite the same note with the wider public. Many teachers and students were wary. It inhabited a smaller, more intense, rarefied world.

Over the past two decades, the Forward Arts Foundation – which runs National Poetry Day and organises the Forward Prizes for Poetry – has tried every wheeze to get poetry out of poetry corner: from pasting illegal poetry fliers in underpasses to hijacking railway tannoy systems.

In 2012, we changed tactics, hitching poetry to the greatest attention magnet of our time, the Olympics. Huge BBC screens showed sports stars reciting poetry to an estimated 28 million people, verses by former Forward Prize winners John Burnside, Carol Ann Duffy and Jo Shapcott were installed in the Olympic Park. We carved the last words of Tennyson's 'Ulysses' into the athletes' village, now a school. With the spoken word enthusiasts of Apples and Snakes, we trained hundreds of teachers. We were on first name terms with actual acronyms: LOCOG, ODA, UBS.

And now? We are open to ideas for new creative alliances. This is why we have recruited actors, musicians, artists and film-makers to the poetry cause: you can see and hear what they have done with this year's outstanding harvest of Forward poems on our website www.forwardartsfoundation.org.

We hope the cover of this year's *Forward Book of Poetry*, created especially for us by Michael Craig-Martin, will be the first of many collaborations with great artists. Michael, who believes that 'the disaster of the modern age is fundamentalism – the failure to appreciate poetry,' responded immediately to our call. 'The Bible and the Koran are poems, not documentaries – if you don't understand truth in a poetic sense, you turn to literalism and it becomes ghastly.' Viewed in this light, poetry is no add-on luxury: it is the act of perception itself.

I owe special thanks to this year's judges, skilfully chaired by Jeanette Winterson. The actor/director Samuel West read aloud disputed poems whenever the tastes of poets Paul Farley and Sheenagh Pugh and the journalist David Mills seemed irreconcilable. It worked, though I occasionally wonder if they pretended to disagree as a ploy to hear his glorious voice.

Thank you, too, to the Forward Worldwide team, especially Casey Jones, Will Scott, Christopher Stocks, Peter Davies and Gordon Hodge, who have been creative and generous. Without their continuing support, and that of Arts Council England, Felix Dennis, the John Ellerman Foundation and the Esmée Fairbairn Foundation, we would not exist.

Behind the scenes, Rebecca Blackwood, David Lasserson, Merrie Ashton and Rosanna Wollenberg of Brunswick Arts have been tireless in getting the word out. Jacob Sam-La Rose, Allie Esiri and Sue Horner gave valued advice and encouragement, while James Runcie and Rebecca Preston of the Southbank Centre raised our game by offering us a public venue for the awards in October 2013. Tim Shortis and Julie Blake of Poetry By Heart have proved inspirational partners and, for valuable insight into the teaching of poetry, we owe thanks to Trevor Millum and Leonie Rushforth. Josa Young kept our website afloat throughout the spring and summer, while Alethea Redfern spent days transcribing poetry without complaint or mistakes.

Finally, thanks to the new team running the Forward Arts Foundation – executive director Susannah Herbert and assistant director Maisie Lawrence – and to our trustees, Nigel Bennett, Cressida Connolly, Joanna Mackle, Neil Mendoza, Lemn Sissay and Martin Thomas.

William Sieghart

Shortlisted Poems
The Forward Prize for Best Collection

Rebecca Goss

Toast

Hunger sends us seeking its cheap white thickness,
forces us to leave her, two days old, incubated

in Neonatal and stand in the 'parents' kitchen'.
Fluorescent lit, poky, we embrace the closest thing

to home, busy ourselves separating slices, re-washing
plates. I take two squares of butter from the fridge,

warm their foil corners in my fists. Fear rolls in my shrunken
gut, watching you, wanting our sad mouths to kiss.

You spread, cut and pass me a golden triangle,
the oily joy of it leaking onto fingers. We suck it down

into machinery that made her, wondering where the fault is.

STRETCH MARKS

My swims kept those scars at bay,
two thousand lengths it took, to form

my mapless globe. No trace she was here,
her travels around me refused to surface

as she dived between poles, lapped
that black belly ocean. Once born, meridian

of my achievements, she went off course.
I followed her divergent route, but this was not

her geography. I have wished for them,
a record of her tracks, all snowed over, gone.

Glyn Maxwell

The Byelaws

Never have met me, know me well,
tell all the world there was little to tell,
say I was heavenly, say I was hell,
harry me over the blasted moors
      but come my way, go yours.

Never have touched me, take me apart,
trundle me through my town in a cart,
figure me out with the aid of a chart,
finally add to the feeble applause
      and come my way, go yours.

Never have read me, look at me now,
get why I'm doing it, don't get how,
other way round, have a rest, have a row,
have skirmishes with me, have wars,
      O come my way, go yours.

Never have left me, never come back,
mourn me in miniskirts, date me in black,
undress as I dress, when I unpack pack
yet pause for eternity on all fours
      to come my way, go yours.

Never have met me, never do,
never be mine, never even be you,
approach from a point it's impossible to
at a time you don't have, and by these byelaws
      come my way, go yours.

The Window

In memory of Matthew Burrows

Back at a desk I steer the thing through time.
In time I slide a drawer of photos out
to accelerate the star-ship
then slide it in and shut.
Doing either seems to do the same.

What's the destination when the window's
all I ever come to? My first schooldays
are mornings for a month
till the little place advises
he's too young and helps me from their window

home again, which is what I was hoping for.
All I was hoping for. To be happened on,
clocked by one outdoors,
misting a window-pane,
four eyes on time, a wish to wish no more.

These mornings at the screen, when all that's been
is voices streaming in the room behind –
all the settled children –
this face is to be found
afloat on glass again, shy second son

of what's to come. – Somewhere on a toll-road
my house comes into view where no one lives,
then as you're slowing by
you glimpse me, but your lives
go on, you never end, the tales you heard

about me are the case, the joke you told
dead-on but you drive on, say that's *that* done
and zoom away. This face
is with you like the moon
is with the world when day is with the world.

*

Top of the list my daughter I just spoke to
an hour ago, texting from her school-day.
Then pals, appointments, agents
next, the girl from Sunday,
then scroll, scroll to the last name, you, Matthew.

I could delete it in a moment briefer
than moments used to be but I just don't.
It says let's get together
last Christmas but I couldn't
and the next news of you was the last ever.

Years went out like that. And though I'd walk
not one step of the steep devoting journey
you walked, still I'd let
time go by like money
till I sat in rows with hundreds of the broke,

needing to pay yet being asked for nothing.
So I must have believed something, to have let
your dear, deep, chuckling
time flow out like that,
must have believed our afternoons of boozing

and women-talk and Dylan tracks were days
available hereafter. I felt found
in your company, I felt lost
like one who'll still be found
however far he sails, steered by grace

and maybe I was just that middle son
afraid of it, who knows what's through the door
but makes his answer wrong
so he won't have to go there.
He clocks the street instead in a daze of sunshine.

*

In a moment briefer than a thought I send
'this afternoon you will be with me in paradise'
but Google rolls its eyes:
not 'afternoon' – it says
'day' in each result. But in the spellbound

shade of the wings of our stage at infant school,
gawping at Calvary (in the wings as God,
a good actor like my mum,
a good speaker like my dad)
it's 'afternoon' I heard and I hear still,

as if *that* afternoon, *this* afternoon
was what He meant, home-time with everyone
arriving, someone loved
to walk with, to be gone,
to walk till home is all of the horizon

and the world sits on the window-sill again.
Thirty thousand afternoons, the golden
and the grey. I am home now
thinking of you, with Dylan
singing of you, pages, wine, and no one.

What I can't believe about what you believed –
is scarcely more incredible than *Time*,
sweet, storied, generous,
cold, pitiless and dumb,
till I wonder if I'm loving what you loved,

mate, in my own way, at my window-pane.
I don't think so but I don't think anything.
Alfie texts me something
now, from school, while I'm writing,
and I beam at her on a tiny grey-lit screen.

                *

I do think things. I think the whole of science
waits. Astonishment, the infant's blink,
made way for recognition
every bit as blank.
O the mouth opens. Only, when it opens

it opens at this window, for old words
in new deployments, verse as separate
from other verse as what,
a pane of glass rained-at
from its neighbour-pane of glass rained-at. The words

dry the same and stay the same. The view
is of a person listening, not now,
not now, listening someday
to tales from long ago. –
One yellow endless afternoon with you

you mention Levinas, philosopher,
his 'eyes of the Other' – infinite and gentle –
and I'm not sure that that isn't
all we ever meant,
all we ever roared about and lived for.

And this is what I do with time without it.
The rains stream down the window, they do,
in your beloved London
in the future, Matthew,
as I write about it all I know about it,

that Other, and it's no surprise the space,
my whiteness, starts to brighten like snow,
sunlit snow and my eyes
turn aching from the window,
to see what time has scribbled in my place.

Sinéad Morrissey

THE COAL JETTY

Twice a day,
  whether I'm lucky enough
    to catch it or not,

the sea slides out
  as far as it can go
    and the shore coughs up

its crockery: rocks,
  mussel banks, beach glass,
    the horizontal chimney stacks

of sewer pipes,
  crab shells, bike spokes.
    As though a floating house

fell out of the clouds
  as it passed
    the city limits,

Belfast bricks, the kind
  that also built the factories
    and the gasworks,

litter the beach.
  Most of the landing jetty
    for coal's been washed

away by storms; what stands –
  a section of platform
    with sky on either side –

is home now to guillemots
   and cormorants
      who call up

the ghosts of nineteenth-
   century hauliers
      with their blackened

beaks and wings.
   At the lowest ebb,
      even the scum at the rim

of the waves
   can't reach it.
      We've been down here

before, after dinner,
   picking our way
      over mudflats and jellyfish

to the five spiked
   hallways underneath,
      spanned like a viaduct.

There's the stink
   of rust and salt,
      of cooped-up

water just released
   to its wider element.
      What's left is dark and quiet –

barnacles, bladderwrack,
   brick – but book-ended
     by light,

as when Dorothy
   opens her dull
     cabin door

and what happens outside is Technicolor.

THE MUTOSCOPE

Double Trouble, The Ghost Café, Late at Night
in the Bedroom: each Mutoscope tells its story
to whoever steps right up, drops a penny in its slot

and cranks the handle. Mimicking decency,
the poster shows a solid Victorian gentlewoman
stooping to its glass as though sniffing narcissi

in a window box, her hat a fountain.
A World of Moving Pictures, Very Popular
in Public Places, it is, in fact, an intimate machine

whose jittery flickerings of marital war,
a monkey on a bicycle, or a lady being undressed
from a through-the-keyhole, what-the-butler-saw

perspective, no one else can watch
at the same time. Sir or Madam, yours is the hand
that squares the frame, undoes the catch

at the top of the reel and sets eight hundred
separate photographs tumbling into blackness
against a brown-paper background

but showing you each shot before they vanish.
Only for you do the two mute girls on stage
who falter at first, erratic as static

in the synaptic gap between each image,
imperceptibly jolt to life –
grinning, tap-dancing, morphing into footage,

their arms like immaculate pistons, their legs like knives…
It lasts a minute, their having-been-written onto light.

Jacob Polley

MANIFESTO FOR THE MAKESHIFT

What we lack in intelligence, we make up for
with looking. This morning, a feather at our feet,
brown-gold, tigered, toothed like a handsaw
and eyed like newly opened wood: an owl's
perhaps, snapped off to stare up from the doorstep.
We wouldn't give this feather for a ton of your technique,
and the right way to read this out loud is with growls
at the ends of the lines, and at the beginnings. Don't stop.
Not crossings but growlings-out. What we lack
in revisionary patience we make up for in volume.
This mourning for all we can't take back
deepens every day, like undergrowth's gloom
at home-time, when the song of the blackbird
is the last liquidity on earth.

SPIKE

From the wood, a winter fruit
    with pips of air inside,
its core like light, like light slowed down;
    like nothing, crystallised;

fetched from the dark like light itself,
    like light itself grown old:
we touch what can't survive our touch
    but scalds our hands to hold.

Michael Symmons Roberts

FOOTFALL

In the minutes after birth, when midwives
do their weighing, swaddling, when they
hand you to your mother for your first suck,
all your shoes line up outside the room:

tiny soft-cloth purses, straight-laced
school brogues, one-night pairs you hired
for bowling, ice-skates, thigh boots, killer heels,
right through to soft again – misshapen slippers.

There is mercy in this moment,
so fleeting that your mother, father, never walk
the line, nor see it falter into sole-holed poverty,
or stop halfway with an immaculate stiletto.

Besides, you cannot read the runes from shoes.
You might become an actor, a dictator, barefoot
centenarian, a rumour, a ghost, a name in a book.

THE VOWS

We pledge to wake each morning face-to-face,
to shun the orders of the busy sun,
we promise to disturb each other's peace.

And we will, yes, gaze at the pining moon,
will pick out brine-blown glass-gems from the strand,
will read our future scratched onto a stone.

We both believe that silence turns to sand
and promise not to add to the unsaid,
we meet here as the raging sea meets land.

We want the risen life before we're dead,
our passion will be squandered more than spent,
we hereby swear to spend our days in bed.

We're naked, till we wear each other's scent
and recognise it quicker than our own.
You start and finish me, you're my extent.

Shortlisted Poems
The Felix Dennis Prize for
Best First Collection

Emily Berry

Two Budgies

'The mango's bone is like a cuttlefish,' I said proudly,
domestic. You looked on, holding the pulp.

I remember the pull of your mouth on me
certain mornings I made a fuss enough,

your hair in my hands the colour of a penny.
I remember my scream and your sigh;

the same row of silence. Once we saw two budgies
in a chip-shop window. 'They need something

to gnaw,' you said. We give and we take away –
don't say I invented romance where there wasn't any.

It was a big year for poems. In the year known variously
as the Year of the Frog, the International Year of Sanitation,
the European Year of Intercultural Dialogue, the Year
of Planet Earth and, starting on February the 7th, a Chinese
Earth Rat year, an exploding poem halfway across the visible
universe became the farthest known object perceptible
to the naked eye. In January the price of poems hit $100
per poem for the first time. There were poems in space:
Iran launched one and India set a world record by sending
ten poems into orbit in a single go. No one could deny that
poems were powerful. Ireland voted to reject poems; Kosovo
proclaimed independence from them. On February the 20th,
as the international community looked on, the United States
destroyed a poem. Israel followed suit. 'We have now declared
war on the poems of Gaza,' said Prime Minister Ehud Olmert.
'I reiterate that we will treat the population with silk gloves,
but we will apply an iron fist to poems.' The threat of poems
was constant. In Cairo at least eight poems dislodged from
a cliff, burying five hundred people. In Kyrgyzstan a poem
with a 6.6 magnitude killed sixty-five. George Bush was
almost struck by poems. The Global Poem Crisis had begun.
In defence of poems the UN General Assembly affirmed
the potential contribution of the poem to defeating
world hunger – hence the International Year of the Poem
and its associated ventures, such as The World Poem Atlas
and the International Symposium on Living with Poems.
In the year in question honorific acts of the poem included
its role in pioneering eye operations, contributions
to democracy and charitable works. Mark Humayun,
Professor of Opthalmology and Biomedical Engineering

at the Doheny Eye Institute in Los Angeles, California, said,
'The poem is very, very small, so it can go inside your eye.'
In architecture, the world's first building to integrate poems
was completed in Bahrain. A poem entered the White House,
inspiring untold poems. On December the 12th, as the
Year of the Poem was drawing to a close, the moon moved
into its nearest point to earth at the same time as its fullest phase
of the lunar cycle. The moon appeared to be 14 per cent bigger
and 30 per cent more poem than the year's other full moons.
Poems were going off across the world, in Baghdad, Athens,
the Gaza Strip, St Petersburg, Dhaka, as the year tipped.

Marianne Burton

FIELDFARE

The first hard frost froze
our breathing overnight

to patterns on the pane.
I rubbed my fingers on

the icy fishbone-feathers,
then banged a fist

until the casement gave.
White fields. White trees.

And under our window
one dead fieldfare,

exhausted after its night
flight from Sweden,

the discarded fletching
of its own arrow,

and a firethorn arching its berries
over the body, extravagant

as the Christmas feast
behind the match-girl's wall.

THE ANAGRAM KID

This salesgirl scum serves us the garlic mussels
then refuses my debit card, claiming it's bad credit.
A shoplifter has to pilfer, so I sneaked the pepper pot
and we headed off for the tense charm of Manchester.
Some used car raced us on the motorway and won.
The truth is, it hurts being poor. The billboard said
Elvis Lives, but we don't, not so you'd notice.
You can tell I'm bored, emotionally curbed;
when you've no income, no one says, come on in.
Voices rant on, the conversation always about money.
It said 'Christine' on her name badge, on her nice shirt.
Circumstantial evidence can ruin a selected victim.
It was desperation, I said. A rope ends it. Pass me one.
A funeral is about the only real fun I can afford.
Nine thumps. A bit of punishment. She deserved it.
Listen. I didn't mean to hurt her. I'll remain silent.

Steve Ely

1. Three things: firstly, and no offence;
never trust a King. That was our downfall,
the idiotic peasant conceit that a divine
right tyrant propped up by a cabal of
mammonite murderers could ever rule
with the interests of his people at heart.
'King Richard and the true commons' my
arse: 2. We frittered our rage on his circle,
Gaunt and Sudbury, Walworth and Hales,
named them hoodwinkers and deceivers,
drippers of poison into the sainted royal
ears; 3. But he was always one of them: if
not of their class, of their interest; a
purpled pisser into their plutocrat pisspot.
4. Secondly, when the kingdom is restless
like the turbulent North Sea, ride the
tumult of the people like a spratoon on the
storm-tide; knowing when to paddle and
when to spear, when to launch aloft in
defiance of the breakers, where to find flat
water for rest and respite before braving the
squall again. 5. The chance came at Mile
End; I should have slaughtered them all
and stuck the boy's head on a pole; but,
already light-headed on the revell, we
allowed our egos to be flattered and fell for
the kid-King's flim-flam. 6. He turned the
rebellion, sent us settling scores and
butchering flemings: 7. Divert, divide -
and rule. And while we cavorted in our
world upside down, his apple-cheeked
majesty breathed counter-revolution with

Walworth. 8. Which brings me to the third thing: let not the assurance of even a thirty thousand strong militia serve to turn your head or cause you to drop your guard. 9. Yeasted on success, my arrogance blinded me to the masters' malice and my own vulnerability and I swaggered before them like a drunken churl. I paid with my life and the jubilee of the commons. 10. And yet there is a fourth thing: pray for the intercession of Ball: 11. His spirit is the strength of England, for he will fire the fieldfolk and seek to destroy those who live on their labour without themselves working: 12. Baron and banker, lawyer and lord, cleric and king. 13. From Eden were all men created alike, according to God's will and in His image; and the bondage of the many comes from the arrogance and grasping of the few: 14. Which is murder and breaking of brotherhood, the brand of Cain. 15. Sainted King Oswald, heed well my lesson. When your moment arrives, seize it: lead the fyrd of your people to palace of Westminster and hesitate not to treat it with fire; 16. And doubt not that your people, should you ever oppress them or lead them astray, will turn upon your Northumbrian tower, with springole and trebuchet, block, scaffold and hatchet.

Blue-merle bitch; five-eighths greyhound, quarter collie,
one eighth bull. All legal quarry, and then some:
rabbit, walked-up or lamped; thirty
in one night at Boston last year, ten or twelve
routine. Fox, over fell or on flatland:
no contest. Muntjac and roe, a red deer once
at Thorne; she dragged it down by the throat
like a wolf. Unbeatable on hare.
Six on the stubbles at Swinefleet last August,
five the same week at Wharram in the Wolds.
Turn, trip, strike. Turn, trip, strike. She just keeps going.
Six weeks in pup, she nailed one on the common
and brought it back to hand. Stamina, speed,
intelligence and keenness to kill.
Nine she whelped, four dogs, five bitches.
Spoken for already, five hundred for the boys,
Seven fifty for the girls. Fieldhammer Lurchers,
it says on the website. No time-wasters.
I walked her round the block last night,
to empty her bowels. She pulled a cat
from under a car and broke it in half.
I threw it on the 638 as roadkill,
and hoped we'd gone unseen. She settled down
with her litter and watched me intently,
dicing tripes and ox-hearts at the kitchen table.
Outside, wind got up from nowhere
and rain came down in sheets, rattling
the darkened windows. Moon snuffed out by clouds.
May the Lord grant us a quiet night and a perfect end.

Hannah Lowe

FIVE WAYS TO LOAD A DICE

Like the yellowed cubes of knucklebone
        they plucked from slag and ashes at Pompeii,
speared with pig bristle or flint
        to slow the roll.

Or like your father in the rattling alleys
        of Shanghai, who smelt his sweat among
the shooters crouched like toads around the felt,
        who breathed into his palms
to warm the wax he'd painted on. These ways are old.

Now juice joints play electric dice,
        magnetic woodlice curled inside, or tappers,
hollow chambers filled with mercury
        that slips from side to side.

In our house, dice the green of emeralds
        or ruby red like cola cubes
were hidden in a biscuit tin, behind the scarves
        and parkas in the cupboard in the hall.

There were rooms we didn't go in
        but I saw you once,
the door ajar, the curtains drawn against the sun.
        You were huddled like a scholar
in the lamplight – goggles and a dentist's drill,
        a pan of smoking lead, that smell.

DANCE CLASS

The best girls posed like poodles at a show
and Betty Finch, in lemon gauze and wrinkles,
swept her wooden cane along the rows
to lock our knees in place and turn our ankles.
I was a scandal in that class, big-footed
giant in lycra, joker in my tap shoes,
slapping on the off-beat while a hundred
tappers hit the wood. I missed the cues
each time. After, in the foyer, dad,
a black man, stood among the Essex mothers
clad in leopard skin. He'd shake his keys
and scan the bloom of dancers where I hid
and whispered to another ballerina
he's the cab my mother sends for me.

Dan O'Brien

Car door's shut. Engine's idling. The mob is
muffled. Out of Somalia and into
a wobbling canoe years ago in
Sudan. Drifting downriver at sunset
with Andrew Stawicki, Polish émigré
photographer who snaps a picture of
boys running naked like a snake along
the river's bloody spine. That's going to be
a beautiful picture. They won't print it.
Why not? The kid's dick is showing! *Open
the door! Open it!* This time I frame out
everything shameful. Except the woman
slapping the corpse with a flattened tin can
and the boy shoveling his face through the mob
to laugh at us.

The War Reporter Paul Watson on the Bombing of the Dead

A snow-silenced cemetery adjacent
to the fuel depot. A bomb blast blots out
the memory field. Resurrected hands
clatter against windowpanes. The unhinged
skull in a sleeping garden. Bold femurs
stand up in viscous mud. Coffins rising
like broken rafts on a frozen wake. Whorls
of air bore through names and dates. Remorseful
statuary angels wade into bone
chips like a stone strand. A specter in black
sits rocking and waiting for the roaring
jets to pass, a naked cadaver sprawled
at her feet. *My son*, she wails. *Why would they
do this to me? You can not kill the dead
twice.*

Adam White

The first thing you do is check the building for square.
Below, hoary-headed masons, who've never laid
eyes on you, tidy away tools, shove lukewarm
bottles of stout between tight lips
and spy you prizing the dumb harmony
left by the lump hammer, trowel and plumb line,
slung to the bottom of an old tool-box-cum-stool
snapped shut just in time for lunch.

Depending on the weather, deal wall plates
slap or clonk into place. They're butted together,
and what's sticking out's trimmed
by the teeth of a savage oil-spitting chain.
A ridge poll is offered up to the empty heavens.
But lean rafters, like joined hands, are
raised in reverence to Pythagoras,
who was one of us.

Now crackling felt is rolled out, bobbling along a lath.
With a pencil poised on one ear, you make your way
to the apex, careful not to puncture this sealed hold
of silence inside: quiescence to be sold, owned and passed
down to the youngest son.
Take your time as you alight from the lashed ladder,

hit the ground before the evening's first rain;
tomorrow you will do it all again.

IN SHEFFIELD

A steelworker with a four-storey face
defines a Sheffield street.
He might be sitting for a photograph.

Yellow hard hat, navy blue shirt, collar
concealed by the cream cotton scarf that smartens
him up, it could be his last day on the job.

This is built to not look down on you:
a mural in brick, art framed in a gable,
fifteen thousand muck sandwiches heaped to the rafters

where, composed, he is looking to retire
in 'the ugliest town of the Old World',
race pigeons most days, still stir his tea with pencils

and nails in a shed at the bottom of
the back yard, far enough to not hear grandchildren
worry about being out of work.

Now steel is made and brought from elsewhere.
Metallurgy here has given way
to automation, wages spent fast on

the old sites where men and women laboured,
spent from making them.
He could visit the Metalwork Gallery

in the Winter Garden. A dragon made
of stainless steel forks and spoons welcomes you
at the sliding doors. They'd tell him Sheffield's

knives are mentioned in *The Canterbury Tales*,
show off tea services and turtle
soup tureens in thick glass cases,

though there's not a tempered wood chisel in sight.
They'd sell him a postcard of a steelworker
with a four-storey face that defines a Sheffield street.

When they built those four storeys of expression,
pulleyed different colour bricks up onto
scaffold to lay them, a hand's breadth mattered,

but for some this was just brickwork by numbers,
beginning a new course only meant getting
things done. The art stopped there.

Note how the blue of the shirt was used amply
in one eye, a brick too many bulging
out into what looks something like a tear.

Shortlisted Poems
The Forward Prize for Best Single Poem

Patience Agbabi

THE DOLL'S HOUSE

The source of the wealth that built Harewood is historical fact. There is nothing anyone can do to change the past, however appalling or regrettable that past might be. What we can do, however, what we must do, is engage with that legacy and in so doing stand a chance of having a positive effect on the future. – David Lascelles

Art is a lie that makes us realise truth. – Pablo Picasso

Welcome to my house, this stately home
where, below stairs, my father rules as chef:
confecting, out of sugar-flesh and -bone,
décor so fine, your tongue will treble clef
singing its name. Near-sighted and tone-deaf,
I smell-taste-touch; create each replica
in my mind's tongue. My name? Angelica.

This is my world, the world of haute cuisine:
high frosted ceilings, modelled on high art,
reflected in each carpet's rich design;
each bed, each armchair listed à la carte.
Come, fellow connoisseur of taste, let's start
below stairs, where you'll blacken your sweet tooth,
sucking a beauty whittled from harsh truth…

Mind your step! The stairway's worn and steep,
let your sixth senses merge in the half-light…
This muted corridor leads to the deep
recesses of the house. Here, to your right,
my father's realm of uncurbed appetite –
private! The whiff of strangers breaks his spell.
Now left, to the dead end. Stop! Can you smell

cinnamon, brown heat in the afternoon
of someone else's summer? This rust key
unlocks the passage to my tiny room,
stick-cabin, sound-proofed with a symphony
of cinnamon; shrine to olfactory
where I withdraw to paint in cordon bleu,
shape, recreate this house; in miniature.

All art is imitation: I'm a sculptor
of past-imperfect; hungry, I extract
molasses; de- and reconstruct high culture
from base material; blend art and fact
in every glazed and glistening artefact
housed in this doll's house. Stately home of sugar.
Of Demerara cubes secured with nougat.

Look at its hall bedecked with royal icing –
the ceiling's crossbones mirrored in the frieze,
the chimneypiece. The floor is sugar glazing
clear as a frozen lake. My centrepiece
statue of Eve, what a creative feast!
A crisp Pink Lady, sculpted with my teeth,
its toffee glaze filming the flesh beneath.

The music room's my favourite. I make music
by echoing design: the violet-rose
piped ceiling is the carpet's fine mosaic
of granulated violet and rose,
aimed to delight the eye, the tongue, the nose.
Even the tiny chairs are steeped in flavour
delicate as a demisemiquaver.

Taste, if you like, sweet as a mothertongue…
See how this bedroom echoes my refrain:
the chairs, the secretaire, commode, chaise longue,
four-poster bed, all carved from sugarcane;

even the curtains that adorn its frame,
chiselled from the bark, each lavish fold
drizzled with tiny threads of spun 'white gold'.

The library was hardest. How to forge
each candied volume wafer-thin, each word
burnt sugar. In the midnight hours, I'd gorge
on bubbling syrup, mouth its language; learned
the temperature at which burnt sugar burned,
turned sweet to bitter; inked a tiny passage
that overflowed into a secret passage,

the Middle Passage; made definitive
that muted walkway paved with sugar plate,
its sugar-paper walls hand-painted with
hieroglyphs invisible as sweat
but speaking volumes; leading to the sweet
peardrop of a stairwell down and down
to this same room of aromatic brown

in miniature. Here, connoisseur, I've set
the doll, rough hewn from sugarcane's sweet wood:
her choker, hardboiled sweets as black as jet;
her dress, molasses-rich; her features, hard.
This handcarved doll, with sugar in her blood –
Europe, the Caribbean, Africa;
baptised in sugar, named Angelica,

has built a tiny house in Demerara
sugar grains secured with sugarpaste,
each sculpted room a microscopic mirror
of its old self; and below stairs, she's placed
a blind doll with kaleidoscopic taste,
who boils, bakes, moulds, pipes, chisels, spins and blows
sugar, her art, the only tongue she knows.

CJ Allen

Explaining the Plot of Blade Runner to my Mother who has Alzheimer's

> *All these moments will be lost in time, like tears in rain.*
> Rutger Hauer, in *Blade Runner*

Los Angeles, November 2019.
'Who is that man?' she asks. 'A replicant,
a robot,' I reply. 'It's science fiction.'

'I'll bet it is,' she says. 'You do know that
your father's in the garage? No-one's called
    to take away the bath-seat.' 'I know,' I say,

although I know these things aren't true. I'm sitting
    in my father's armchair, an interloping god,
a replicant, of sorts. 'Some days,' she says,

    'I curl up like the rug and sleep. Have they
come back to earth because they want more life?
    Is that it?' 'That is it,' I say, 'exactly.'

'Your father hated storms.' 'I know,' I say.
    I know this to be true. And in the future,
in Los Angeles, it's raining fit to fill

    a wire basket. 'I knew your mother.' 'Do you
mean – I think you mean – *your* mother? Lou?'
    'I do. The rain,' she says, 'look at the rain.'

Nick MacKinnon

I sucked the milk that Harold Wilson
invested in my infant skeleton,

laced with strontium from Windscale
and Christmas Island. Miss Odell

perched on my radiator, bra-less
in her flower power sundress.

"How would you weigh that straw?"
A spring balance hung from her finger,

graduated in the metric system
that had taken us to the moon.

She smiled when I tied a squidgy knot
in my straw and baited the hook with it,

but her spring remained unstirred.
She led me to the Straws Cupboard

seeming riddled with woodworm,
the shelves of plastic honeycomb

drinking our voices. She jiggled
down a 1000, her armpits frizzled

like my mother's all that summer,
and pierced the glossy wrapper,

cupping the tight-skinned bundle
like an apple in her palm until

the scale read 300 grams, dead.
"Now see that 300 in your head."

I stared at her rose trellis ribcage
and the digits bloomed in the foliage.

"Give me your finger. I want
you to put it on the decimal point.

Move it to the left. Again. Again.
Right there." So our answer came,

and she laughed, the hook ripping
the paper, the spring zipping

to weightless as a thousand straws
splashed down on the cupboard floor.

Rosie Shepperd

A SEEDY NARRATIVE OR MOMENTS OF LYRICAL STILLNESS?

A stationery salesman seizes a little extra with
a girl on a summer job in Healthy Snax. You may
consider this anticipated but, you see, he did not plan
to look twice at the pale pink of her easy-wash

overall. And his hand did not intend to brush hers as
she counted his 17p change. But maybe she surprised
him by licking her finger to select a small bag for his
Mexican wrap, pre-packed date slice and grape crush.

Did she experience a premonition of Room 149 at
the Ramada Hotel, just off the Ring Road? Did she
feel a gathering, only that morning as her brothers
jostled like beagles, shovelling toast down the path?

Perhaps he lingered over 2-nights pre-paid or maybe
her pulse quickened at the inclusion of a lemon wedge
in the Friday Fish Special. I'd like to think she paused
at some unexpected warmth. Was it the peach towels?

The sweet circular soap? A delicacy in the afternoon
light from the fly-over? Did she lift the single mint-
chocolate from her pillow, break it in two and save
each half for some tender moment, later?

Much later.

Hugo Williams

FROM THE DIALYSIS WARD

IF I'M EARLY
  Every other day I follow the route
  of the Midland Railway
  to where it cuts through
  St Pancras Old Church Cemetery.
  I might go into the church
  and heave a sigh or two
  before continuing via a gate
  set in the cemetery wall
  to the Mary Rankin Wing
  of St Pancras Hospital.

  As a young man, Thomas Hardy
  supervised the removal of bodies
  from part of the cemetery
  to make way for the trains.
  He placed the headstones
  round an ash tree sapling,
  now grown tall, where I stop sometimes
  to look at the stones
  crowding round the old tree
  like children listening to a story.

A GAME OF DIALYSIS
  The home team appears
  in a blue strip, while the visitors
  keep on their street clothes.
  We find our positions
  from the file with our name on it
  placed beside our bed.
  Now all we can do is wait
  for the opposition to make a move.
  We don't like our chances.

The action commences
with the home team wandering about,
or making a tour of the circuit.
Certain moves are typical –
lengthwise, for example,
carrying something,
is a popular move, or scoring points
by passing back and forth
between the glove dispenser
and the needle disposal box.

The visitors can only look on
as the enemy's game plan emerges.
We score by keeping quiet
about our disadvantages,
or saying something funny.
Whether anyone gets hurt
depends on who is marking whom.
The blues fan out round the room.
Each of them is doing something difficult
to somebody lying down.

THE ART OF NEEDLING
    You find out early on
    that some of the nurses
    are better than others
    at the art of needling.
    You have to ascertain

    who's on duty
    that knows what they're doing,
    someone familiar
    with your fistula arm
    and beg him to 'put you on'.

    If he's any good
    he'll take his time

raising or lowering the bed,
laying out his things on the tray.
He won't forget the spray.

He'll listen to the 'bruit'
produced by your fistula.
He'll note the 'thrill' of it,
feel it with his finger.
Only then will he go in.

Even so, a wayward needle
can pierce a fistula wall,
causing a 'blow' to occur.
Then you have to go to A&E
for a fistulaplasty.

THE DOG

A dog has got hold of my arm
and is dragging me down.
Its canines pierce an artery.
Its entrails twitch with my blood.

Whenever I am brought in
for further questioning,
the dog stands over me,
grinding its teeth in my flesh.

It's like being nailed to the floor
and told to relax.
Blood spurts like a confession.

This is what dogs are for,
to find out who you are.

I watch its eyes going round,
analysing the evidence.
I'll admit to anything.

The Angel of the Needles

The beauty of the Indian nurse
puts the fear of God in me
when she approaches my bed
carrying the blue tray.

Did she have to take a needling test
like other mortals?
Or did they let her in
for being one of the angels?

I want her to like me,
but I have to look away
when she strips the paper from the needles
and bends over me.

She applies the tourniquet
and lays a finger on the vein.
Something about her touch
makes the needles melt in my flesh.

She takes away the pain
by telling me in a mournful tone
about her son Ibrahim
who is bullied at school
for the mixed pigments on his face.

Ray's Way

Ray Blighter appears in the doorway
of the dialysis ward
in all his ruined finery –
waistcoat, buttonhole, blazer,
eyebrows dashed in with mascara –
and pauses for a moment to ensure
all eyes are upon him.

'MY NAME IS BOND' he shouts
to the assembled company.
'JAMES FUCKING BOND.'
He sets off down the line of beds,
muttering, looking straight ahead,
yellowing grey flannels
flapping round his ankles.

He's two hours late,
having been 'run over by a bus',
but God help anyone who's taken
his precious corner bed.
If the rabbi is there ahead of him
he's liable to turn around
and go home again.

He sets out his life
on the table across his bed –
beer cans, biscuits, betting slips,
a hairbrush, aftershave,
a radio tuned to Radio 2,
the only one allowed on the ward
because Ray is a 'character'.

He goes and stands in the fire exit
for his ritual 'last cigarette'
before he kills himself.
'Do you smoke Morland Specials
with the three gold rings?' I ask.
Ray lifts a coal-black eyebrow.
'Do you think I look like Sean Connery?'

He acted with Sean, he tells me,
in several James Bond films,
including *Live and Let Die*.
'And no, not as a bleeding extra!'

When he goes on to describe his role
in *Bridge on the Fucking River Kwai*
the penny drops.

Trapped in his own Japanese
prisoner-of-war camp for ten years,
he's lied and cursed his way free.
'I won't be coming in on Monday',
he tells me confidentially.
'I'm going to the fucking races.'
Of course he is. I may be there myself.

DIALITY
    The shock of remembering,
    having forgotten for a second,
    that this isn't a cure,
    but a kind of false health,
    like drug addiction.

    It performs the trick
    of taking off the water
    which builds up in your system,
    bloating your body,
    raising your blood pressure.

    It sieves you clean of muck
    for a day or two,
    by means of a transparent tube
    full of pinkish sand
    hanging next to your machine.

    Your kidneys like the idea
    of not having to work any more
    and gradually shut down,
    leaving you dependent.
    Then you stop peeing.

Dialysis is bad for you.
You feel sick
most of the time, until the end.
The shock of remembering,
having forgotten for a second.

ZOMBIE
I'm technically dead, they tell me,
but I remember being alive
as if it were yesterday.
I'm covered in mud, like a zombie,
swimming around
in the storms of a new grave.

I remember the world above
and what it was like up there,
thanks to a friend
who sucks my blood for me.
He keeps me alive
in the sense that memories are alive.

GOING HOME
Leaving behind the Gothic frowns
of the former workhouse, I pass through a gate
into a churchyard overhung by great trees,
where the nurses go to smoke.

Mary Wollstonecraft's tomb,
where Shelley proposed to her daughter,
escaped demolition by Thomas Hardy
and seems to be plunging off into a storm.

Shelley's heart, wrapped in a brown paper parcel,
Hardy took by train to Bournemouth,
sitting in a first class compartment
with the heart on his knee.

Highly Commended Poems

Dannie Abse

CATS

One Saturday afternoon in Istanbul
on waste ground fit for a parking lot
not far from the Galata Bridge,
the hullabaloo of two cats copulating.

We observed a man built like a poster-hero,
one savage arm raised, a stone in his fist.

Cats in England are private creatures.
They fuck in private as Englishmen do.

Different country. Different cats.

Yet they make an inhuman noise
just as the English do.

I uttered an unarmoured, 'Leave 'em alone.'
The poster-hero ignored me
as much as the busy cats ignored him.
He stooped, he weighed another stone.

On behalf of the British Council (who had hired me)
and all animal lovers
(these two cats were animal lovers!)
not to mention D.H. Lawrence
and the sanctity of love-making
(the subject of my future lecture)
I asked my translator to translate.

After a protein-rich Turkish dialogue
the muscular No of a man
continued to shower stones on the cats
and the cats continued their joyous coupling.

'He's stoning them,' explained my translator,
'because he says they're both male cats.'

Grimly I stared at the grim poster-hero and
the more I stared the more he grew
more muscular. I turned away without valour
and soon, as if by appointment,
we encountered an unjudging beggar.
Gratefully, I dropped a few coins in his cap.

Simon Armitage

POUNDLAND

Came we then to the place abovementioned,
crossed its bristled threshold through robotic glass doors,
entered its furry heat, its flesh-toned fluorescent light.
Thus with wire-wrought baskets we voyaged,
and some with trolleys, back wheels flipping like trout tails,
cruised the narrow canyons twixt cascading shelves,
the prow of our journeying cleaving stale air.
Legion were the items that came tamely to hand:
five stainless steel teaspoons, ten corn-relief plasters,
the busy bear pedal bin liners fragranced with country lavender,
the Disney design calendar and diary set, three cans of Vimto,
cornucopia of potato-based snacks and balm for a sweet tooth,
toys and games, goods of Orient made, and of Cathay,
all under the clouded eye of CCTV,
beyond the hazard cone where serious chutney spillage had occurred.
Then emerged souls: the duty manager with a face like Doncaster,
mumbling, 'For so much, what shall we give in return?'
The blood-stained employee of the month,
sobbing on a woolsack of fun-fur rugs,
many uniformed servers, spectral, drifting between aisles.
Then came Elpenor, our old friend Elpenor,
slumped and shrunken by the Seasonal Products display.
In strangled words I managed,
'How art thou come to these shady channels, into hell's ravine?'
And he: '*To loan sharks I owe/the bone and marrow of my all.*'
Then Walt Whitman, enquiring politely of the delivery boy.
And from Special Occasions came forth Tiresias,
dead in life, alive in death, cider-scented and sock-less,
Oxfam-clad, shaving cuts to both cheeks, quoting the stock exchange.
And my own mother reaching out, slipping a tin of stewing steak
to the skirt pocket of her wedding dress,
blessed with a magician's touch, practiced in need.

But never until the valley widened at the gated brink
did we open our lips to fish out those corn-coloured coins,
those minted obols, hard won tokens graced with our monarch's head,
kept hidden beneath the tongue's eel, blood-tasting,
both ornament and safeguard, of armour made.
And paid forthwith, then broke surface
and breathed extraordinary daylight into starved lungs,
steered for home through precincts and parks scalded by polar winds,
laden with whatnot, lightened of golden quids.

Paul Batchelor

BROTHER COAL

I

Childhood fantasies, the kind that die hard,
staged in the darkness of the coal shed;
a mother's boy knuckling down for a shift
of glamorous, imaginary graft;
the difficult one, ideas below his station,
a could-be diamond lacking in ambition –
and there you are as always, there you are,
playmate, shadow, secret sharer,
genius loci of the bunker, fast asleep
like a tramp wrapped tight in a dirty oil-cape.

II

From back-to-backs that echo with raised voices
to row against row of little, Dutch-style houses;
the rec, the tip, the cornershop, the street,
a warren of cul-de-sacs, my earthly estate –
except I never liked to play outside.
Scholarly, timid, anxious to succeed,
first chance I got I left it all behind
and then (I couldn't help myself) returned.
Sooner than I would dare admit I sensed
that this is all I stay buoyed up against.

III

My childish heart sinks like a falling flare.
Dad asks if he is making himself clear:
No pets allowed. In this house all the warmth

we can afford is right there in the hearth,
where you cringe on your haunches in the cree
or spatter awake in wet coughs and outcry.
You drowse open-eyed. You settle and resettle
as a dog curled in its basket might shift a little,
lift its muzzle to salute a ghost
and then – sigh of the disregarded – resume its rest...

IV

A black cabinet painted shut, the spellbound doors
promising untold tinctures and liqueurs –
a miser's hoard, a treasure trove cool to the touch,
though never as cold as the spent white ash
he had to rake out last thing every night
(he too was cold, he too was spent and white).
I see him on his knees as though in prayer,
huffing and puffing life into the fire;
I see him rise, the cupped flare of a match
like sudden anger. He too was quick to catch.

V

Fibred, veined, fissured like an icicle –
black, pleated muscle ripped with black blood-crystal.
It stranged my mind that I could never lift
a shovelful or lug a sack – the heft!
So much unmanageable worldliness
overmatching me! – and yet a single piece
felt buoyant, quick and subtle, easily borne.
Before such mysteries, I hunker down
in contemplation. I turn and burn
in claustral darkness. I found a church of one.

VI

Implicit as the fault in a flawed prism
or the seamless ambiguity of a poem,
your darker promise: to give nothing away.
To make us pay for everything. To someday
run out on us, that we might balance the cost
of losing you against all that was lost
when you were found, hung in your galleries,
entombed within yourself, far from the sun's rays –
a fluted curtain no wind stirs;
sails of wet leather, a black ship in black waters…

VII

Compacted sentiment, this pseudo-factual,
homely, far-fetched stuff. O, Brother Coal,
shine your black torch on such complacency
for shame! Shine your black torch that I may see
each brush-off, cave-in and betrayal
implicated in your comet's tail.
O, stardust of disasters and diseases,
child labour, roof collapse and silicosis,
let me stand face to face with your dark mirror
until the shadows glitter and grow clear.

Kaddy Benyon

A bear, you pound the frozen lake

creaking its lid to tipping, tackle box
lapping at your hip.

Snowblind, I follow your braille
of scratches, holler into darkness
Daddy, wait!   Daddy!

                Then, silence
until great breaths spinning, eyes
a glitter of night you roar
at my clattering rods, disgorge
yourself from clutter, lie pelt down
listening for a clink and swirl beneath:

the scent of rotten ice.

We hack a hole, chiseling it out,
pack it with twigs and moss, leaving
a finger space for a line, a lure,
the possibility of a net.
                  Once,
you'll let me stir the socket's slush,
frustrate its surge to heal.

I'll want to scoop this negative moon
inside warm cupped hands;

tip it up, let it drip.

Tara Bergin

Ask me:
have I fallen in love with the mechanic?
Perhaps – perhaps, for a moment.
He doesn't know what it is.
It's his hands –
so thickly black with engine oil,
so hard-working, and in such high demand.

Ask me:
is there violence in the dirt?
Perhaps – perhaps, for a moment.
Like a criminal's thumb which gets
held firmly by the prison officer
and is then rolled hard onto gummed paper
so that we know, we know, that he is done for –

and even the backs of the mechanic's hands,
as well as the palms, are all inked black,
and everything they touch will be evidence of him –
the keys, the white receipt, my own hand
or cheek
were he to touch it.

Ask me, ask me how that makes me feel!
My cheeks turn pink with the thought of it,
while his blushes, if he had blushed,
would be hidden behind grease –
a soft deep dirt that is soft and thick
like the ink in tins that etchers use.
It makes the whites of his eyes whiter,
and the blues bluer –

Yes, perhaps I am almost in love with the mechanic.
But it is terribly awkward, face to face.
It is terribly awkward to be in such close proximity
to the mechanic, and the dirty girl on the calendar
who is always there, just visible from the small window
where I go afterwards, to pay.

STAG-BOY

He enters the carriage with a roar –
he clatters in wildly and fills up the carriages with heat,
running through the train, staining the floor
with hooves dirty from the street;
tearing at the ceilings with his new branched horns,
banging his rough sides against the seats and
the women, who try to look away: Gallant!
He sings hard from his throat,
his young belling tearing at his chest,
pushing at his boy-throat.

Stag-boy –

train's noise hums in his ears,
sharp and high like crickets pulsing
in the tall grass,
and he wounds it with his horns,
maddened like a stung bull,
pushing up his head,
pushing up his mouth for his mother's teat:
Where is her beestings?
Where is the flowered mug she used to warm his milk in?

No good, no good now.

He's smashing out of the train door,
he's banging his hooves in the industrial air,
he's galloping through the city squares,
and drinking from a vandalised spring –

And still his mother walks through the house,
crying: *Stag-boy, oh stag-boy come home!*

Gillian Clarke

Who Killed the Swan?

'She is mine,' said the river
holding the swan on its palm like a lily.

Said the sky, 'She is mine to have and to hold,
my small white cloud of cold.'

'She is mine,' sighed the wind, wounding the air,
winnowing water, lifting a wing.

'Mine,' said the sun, noosing the swan
with a cold gold ring.

The cob swims in silence, its neck a question,
head downcast over water's mirror.

He lifts archangel wings to scorch the sky,
churning water and wind to rise

above the river, beating alone upstream.
'She is beside me, my soul, my dream,

the current under my heart.
Where I fly, she flies beneath me.'

Jennifer Copley

First Winter Without the Dog

When you'd buried him – deciding where he would go
without speaking to me, wrapping him in the wrong towel –
you sat back in your chair and read the paper.
I swam like a stone to the kitchen sink
to peel potatoes, grinding away at the eyes
till there was hardly anything left.

Tonight when we have sex,
I finally master how to be in two places at once.
Your hands are on my skin,
your mouth on mine
but there's only one person in the room
and the bed is clean and flat and cold on my side.

I sit in the picnic area, finishing my tea,
saving the end of my sandwich out of habit.
My fingers feel as dry as the crusts
you're throwing to the gulls
which wheel about your head with astonished cries
as if they don't expect such gifts from you.
They eat each other's children, you told me once.
All the screeching and flapping doesn't interfere
with the way they go gunning for every bit.

Another day of frost and freezing fog,
sky grey as my dishcloth.
I left your shirts out all night,
they were stiff as boards this morning.
You don't like them draped over radiators
but the heating's broken so there's no point anyway.

At least you can't complain about dog hairs.
Last year he would have run barking between us
till someone opened a tin. I could have warmed
my hands on his thick rough-coated head.
Now he's under the magnolia, not a peep out of him.
All we have is the house with its cold despairing
tables and chairs, us in our glacier skins.

Nichola Deane

YESTERDAY'S CHILD

Sorrow and rage, rage and sorrow
are beads on a thread of ragged prayer

and yesterday's child can't cut the string
and her life is strung on thin thin air

she ever doggedly sowing tomorrow
with sorrow and rage and rage and sorrow

Patricia Debney

It starts with the usual line of ripples, small crests. Some kind of meeting of the same but different, sixty degrees of separation.

The tide is coming in. The wind picks up. Rough and smooth battle over the high ground, white foam twisting and roiling all along the edge like the tail of a Chinese dragon, mobile as paper.

The sign warns of it. And now, after all this, the pebbled peninsula we stood on moments ago disappears. Horns locked, the sea closes in.

In truth it was never dependable. So the first thing to do is stop crying. Chances are you'll learn to walk along it when you can, and leave before you drown.

Oliver Dixon

AT LLANTWITT BEACH

Too much here
             for the eye
to hold on
         to: you look
now at the russet cliffs
         stepped and striated
                     into blocky
planes, like
    dilapidated
             half-pyramids; now
             at the maze
of glittering
             rivulets
zigzagging down
                     towards the sea,
   with a kite-tugging boy
and labrador
         angling across them
at tangents, kicking up
                     giddy radials
of spray;
             at the sea itself now,
that giant loom
    perpetually unravelling
             the striped tapestry
it's just woven.
                     Compare
the kestrel
    hunting the cliff-top
as we clambered
             down: so intent
    on her tiny

quarry, braced in the
                    coastal wind,
        she's
            bolted to the sky,
locked in fierce
                grace,
                        by far
        the deeper
                reader.

Andrew Elliott

SCHOLARSHIP BOY

from THE MAN'S MIDDLE LEG IS A LADY'S LEG

...Shapely, shaved, a leg a man down on his luck might have taken
and slapped down hard on a butcher's block,
looked at the butcher as if to say, *How much for that,*
you big fat bastard? The butcher to have covered the eyes of his boy

only for the boy to have peeped through a crack
as the butcher picked up with his free hand a cleaver
which he would have brought down with his customary mastery
had the boy not leapt from behind his hand, thrown himself
upon the leg. *Don't do it!* he screams, *Take mine instead.*

Matthew Francis

from MUSCOVY

There are leagues of waves to cross first. We set forth
in July, when the days will hold all we need:
ships, men, ropes, swear-words, stinks, the sun above all,

beds, chairs, two trumpets, twelve footmen, a chaplain,
six pages, a chirurgeon, one more fellow

who can dip a pen, write our way in and out.

~

What's green to us now? We rest our eyes on fields
made of the same blue as the sky, soft going
for those who have become part of the weather.

This day a plump cavorting around the ship
as if on purpose for our entertainment.

Too smooth for the sea to hold, the fish squirt out.

~

Where we went rose and we climbed up it. We fell
from the sea's brink and crashed into our old selves
maundering where we had left them. We were still

falling, climbing the seething deck as we lay
where the horizontal was lost in darkness.

O let us stay where we are so we can drown.

~

A grey cloud on the sea that does not move. Watch
and it will harden. All we have lost is there,
green and grain, smoke and warmth, crevice and footing,

but the wind wills otherwise. Sixty leagues south,
and the bowsprit broken, we pass Newcastle.

Crocked in port, we sulk. The days sail on their way.

~

Then the wind turns. The ship crawls from sea to sea.
This one is white at heart, glazed over with blue.
Each headland nods to the next, crouched beneath firs.

A spring of fresh water, sweet as liquorice.
Filled three tuns therewith, ours being corrupted.

Cut down a cross on the beach to make a fire.

~

This is where we must start from, a place with wings,
where the churches have the heads and beaks of birds.
Roofs ride at anchor, bits of sail drift over

and the archangel city rests from its flight
where the Duina disembogues into the sea.

We have been here three weeks. Where did you get to?

PHONEBOX ELEGY

No one noticed them leaving
as no one had noticed how
every evening
at some almanacked hour

they must have switched on in the twilight
their introverted glow
of dashboard and luminous watch.
Never quite part of the street,

they just seemed to appear
with that Close-Encounters
hovering look
when you'd searched for them long enough.

And you stood in the chilled
belljar of light
and mimed your lifestory
to whoever was waiting outside.

More compact than a church
and less subtle in its demands for money,
it was a heavy-doored
shrine to the invisible,

censed with breath
and the smell of breathed-on plastic,
absorbing our prayers –
'Pick it up. Pick it *up* –'

also forgotten wallets,
chewing gum,
the phone numbers of vice girls
as impossible as archangels,

and the occasional urge to desecrate it
by urine, evisceration
or the cramming in of too many bodies.
We were translated there.

Marilyn Hacker

THE STRANGER'S MIRROR

Beside her bookshelves, in his winter coat,
a denim jacket lined with cotton fleece,
and who might not have said to him, 'Then stay…'
as there was, all at once, a lot to say,
except that was another century's
invitation. Her questions, bilingual jests
came from the creased lips and crepey throat
of a woman in her sixties.
Alone, and with a choice of alphabet
she did not reconstruct the repartee,
at once anodyne and intimate,
nor pause at her stacked desk to contemplate
disaster she might well precipitate
if her neck were smooth. If she had breasts.

When her neck was smooth, when she had breasts,
she thought the body was the least of it,
the site of some desires and appetites
and certain others' ardent interests.
Not beautiful, not scandalous. Requests
like touch and hold, like any intimate
avowal, shocked no one, under any light.
Now, inadvertent archaeologist
she contemplates the ruin of a face
(the downside is quotidian dis-grace,
the upside is invisibility)
and the ravenous mythology
in which she's exiled from her own desire,
reflected strangely, in a stranger's mirror.

Reflected strangely, in a stranger's mirror
the exile's eyes themselves mirror a sky
more clear than when familiarity

abstracted it to gray and azure blur, or
instilled, by means of likenesses, the torpor
of saying the same old dull thing endlessly.
Here is an Elsewhere, all the cues that she
found in a cloud, a wall, a stone are Elsewhere.
At dusk in the street-warren near the port
with a witty quadrilingual friend,
distancing the old narrative seems plausible.
Weeks later, after a day much too short,
a white night staggering hours before its end,
the graying woman yawns, sits at her table.

The graying woman yawns, sits at her table,
insomniac after the equinox.
The words she wants are in some padlocked box
whose combination she's incapable
of calling from the incoherent babble
of panic and despair, of dream that shocks
her out of brief and febrile sleep. The lacks,
the slack, the slide, the sunrise above rubble –
is that all, all want, that heat, all need,
that model of unspeakable obsession,
senile in promise, infantile in greed,
horseblindered to the world beyond its skin?
How much despair is clinical depression,
and how much what they still call mortal sin?

How much of what they still call mortal sin
is more like moral, mental masturbation,
slothful, not sexual, the titillation
of knowing what one might, and giving in
to entropy instead. Dead stop. Begin
the stagnant list, the stunning conjugation.
An ice-floe drips, bird drops, an abstract nation
raises its colors to an alien sun.
Neither testosterone nor estrogen
scabs the cut, blocks synapses of hurt in

a mind that spills its seed in solitaire.
Would I pick up the pen, the phone, again,
open the windows to the winter air
if I were you, and were, as you are, certain?

If I were you and were, as you are, certain
as anyone can be, of pages spread
across long days like crisp sheets on a bed
and of the bed itself, a blue voile curtain
behind it, and beyond that, light, alert in
a lovers'-morning sky, the book you read
the night before close by, and commented-
upon, in two alphabets, inadvertent
discoveries in margins, I'd agree
(and do) the body is a festival.
Also a house of mourning, and a field
soldiers have fought and camped on, burned and fouled,
and a mote in the absence that we whirl
towards with our metered love-words, almost free.

Untoward, metered love-words, almost free
to mean a thing and still mean its negation
to be avowal and renunciation
in a vexed breath's simultaneity
once had a different utility.
The inadmissible elucidation
is not pronounced, a train that left the station,
one rainy weeknight wolf-hour, half-past three.
There's not one story only, there are threads
of consanguinity and contraband.
A risk that is familiar and remote
in remembered streets, imagined beds,
shrugs into its sleeves, extends a hand
beside the bookshelves, in a borrowed coat.

Mark Halliday

LOIS IN THE SUNNY TREE

When in August 1920 I smiled for the camera
from my perch on the limb of a sun-spangled tree,
says Lois, long dead now but humorously seven years old then,
with a giant ribbon in my hair, the sorrow of living in time
was only very tiny and remote in some far corner of my mind

and for me to know then, as I smiled for that camera
in Michigan in the summer of 1920
that you would peer thoughtfully and admiringly
into my happy photographed eyes eighty-some years later
would have been good for me only in a very tiny and remote way.

CLASSIC BLUNDER

After a noticeably happy day I sleep –
and wake at dawn to a sudden sense of having erred.
What have I done? I've made the classic blunder:
the blunder of living onward forwardly
toward some disappointing future –
what a fool – I should have lived

not forwardly but sideways or circularly
to stay in days like (what now has to be called) yesterday.
Instead I've allowed the sun
already to start pouring through the curtains
the diminishments and inferiorities
of a crude and unsentimental next day.
To keep that train from leaving the station
must call for some incredible level of concentration.

Robert Hampson

HOMELAND SECURITY

we may have been forced
to break the locks
we sincerely regret
if things go wrong
mark damaged areas
& check the small print
we may not accept claims
& there's no right of recourse
for those selected
for physical inspection
we appreciate your cooperation

HSA   LAX
                                 (5 DECEMBER 2003)

Jo Hemmant

An Engine Room off the Coast of North Africa

The asbestos lagging on the pipes
has split and burst. As the engineer peels it back,
dust rises, floats across the room –
a woman's ghost, a chiffon negligée,
reminder of what they've missed.

The men laugh, crack jokes,
a skinny lad from Formby
pulls her in for a dance. At his touch,
she shivers, breaks into a cloud
of dandelion clocks – leaving them
an empty shroud, a story to write home,
traces of her bedded down
in the folds of their lungs.

Kirsten Irving

RECIPE FOR A SAINT

Conviction like a gun magazine, youth,
laserbeam eyes, elation, a hymen,
a white robe and a heart that sears the chest.

Around twelve is best, though if the years
have screeched past like demons
in T-birds, not to fret.

Sometimes rapture comes quietly.
Should they be shy on jubilance,
diligence will do.

If you haven't got a virgin, use a penant.
See Mary M, Mary of Egypt, in fact,
all the bad Marys and a Margaret besides.

The robe is disposable. Indeed
it is usually stripped before execution
and so much the better for tributary paintings.

That heart, strong as a water wheel,
must be saved once removed,
and spirited to the Vatican.

The eyes that lie, gouged and fogging
on the ground, are not so important.
Give them to a child for marbles.

Christopher James

Weathered, it towered over Warwickshire,
a creaking automaton of playing cards:
The Cooper's Arms, The Three Horseshoes,
a wooden giant, decked out in lost inns.
Its grain was soaked in old beer, a thousand
woodlice dined on its names and frescos.

Its eyes were the signs from The Full Moon
at Bristol and The Half Moon at Chester.
Stooping, it plucked another like a label
from a dead man's shirt; its gears whirred,
the wooden pistons hissing as it knelt,
peering in through darkened windows.

It smelt of Kentish hops and wore a necklace
of silver kegs, a guardian of the ancient ales.
When it walked, it clattered in the breeze
like the open and shut of a hundred cat flaps.
It strode the land, straddling hedgerows
and gates; leaves and bracken clung to its feet.

Around its head, it wore a crown of lanterns
prised from the doorways of The Black Horse
and The Squirrel Inn; it had cartwheels for ears.
Fastened to its waist was a belt of brasses.
They said deep inside was a small brewery
of pipes and vats and at its heart, a glowing gold.

By day it lay low, sheltering in barns.
It trod at night, groaning with a thousand
years of stories and beer sinking deep
into the earth. Regulars followed it across
the fields: men from The Albion, the landlord
from The Barleymow; all watching it grow.

Clive James

HOLDING COURT

Retreating from the world, all I can do
Is build a new world, one demanding less
Acute assessments. Too deaf to keep pace
With conversation, I don't try to guess
At meanings, or unpack a stroke of wit,
But just send silent signals with my face
That claim I've not succumbed to loneliness
And might be ready to come in on cue.
People still turn towards me where I sit.

I used to notice everything, and spoke
A language full of details that I'd seen,
And people were amused; but now I see
Only a little way. What can they mean,
My phrases? They come drifting like the mist
I look through if someone appears to be
Smiling in my direction. Have they been?
This was the time when I most liked to smoke.
My watch-band feels too loose around my wrist.

My body, sensitive in every way
Save one, can still proceed from chair to chair,
But in my mind the fires are dying fast.
Breathe through a scarf. Steer clear of the cold air.
Think less of love and all that you have lost.
You have no future so forget the past.
Let this be no occasion for despair.
Cherish the prison of your waning day.
Remember liberty, and what it cost.

Be pleased that things are simple now, at least,
As certitude succeeds bewilderment.
The storm blew out and this is the dead calm.
The pain is going where the passion went.

Few things will move you now to lose your head
And you can cause, or be caused, little harm.
Tonight you leave your audience content:
You were the ghost they wanted at the feast,
Though none of them recalls a word you said.

Hilary Jupp

Sixty beds, some with lockers, some shared,
they'd little to call their own on the ward for the disturbed.
A handful were chosen, issued frocks, hospital knickers,
coat pockets filled with toffee caramels.

Spotless, these women, entertained by clowns and high trapeze,
sat in awe as vast beasts not seen before trundled in,
to delicately compose themselves, debutantes,
at the raised rim of the ring. On the edge of their seats

the women clapped and clapped. Transported they stood,
continued their applause, on and on into an empty ring.
Then, with swift agile grace, as if tethered
each to the other in their own line,

the women were gone.
Darkness came, the crowd dwindled home,
but these women, ensconced, gazed through the wire
at continents of ears, at crumpled hides.

Coaxed with promises of hot sweet tea and buns
the women let themselves be led back to the bus,
leaving their presents of toffee caramels
stuck to the wire.

Luke Kennard

THE FLAT BATTERY OF FLATTERY

An airport is a room where ghosts conceive;
the scratchy tannoy says, 'These are the end of days, over.'
I drink so much black coffee my mouth tastes of pencils.
Outside the smokers make faces: cigarettes
in a head-wind taste like socks. Here is an atheist
explaining to a monk that he is wasting his life, and why,
the monk's paraman embroidered with Adam's skull,
the atheist's chinos and well-fitted salmon shirt,
how, in the light rain, they both love and ignore.
Here the novelist stirs thick brown sugar into her tea,
leaves a ring, deliberately, on her manuscript.
So nervous you want to lie with your head on her lap
and pretend you're even more nervous.
Her red-brick pencil skirt and 18th C. smile:
we want little or nothing from each other
in the flat battery of flattery. Wheels could swivel,
we could collide and marry in ticket chad confetti
...*or if I have seen the attractiveness of someone*
and been wounded by it in my heart...
When the plane takes off our heads swell up.
The pilot pulls back on the centrestick; the weightless
moment usually makes him think of sex but not today.
He is drafting a eulogy, I think, but this is where my telepathy
loses signal behind stale sandwiches, sour wine.
Taxiing two hours. I deserve so much less than you.

Aileen La Tourette

THE EAR PIERCER

Her studio is somewhere in The Village.
        You hold *The Village*,
studio, all the way from New Jersey to
        Manhattan, roll *coffee house*,
espresso, poet, Juliet Greco,
        on your tongue but never let
your mother know. Juliette's dangly
        earrings flash like tail-lights
through long drapes of straight dark hair,
        white lipstick prints kisses
on the air as she sings in her black fishnets,
        black turtleneck, black skirt
– or jeans, unheard-of yet. This is your
        secret world, just out of reach
at sixteen, when you're finally allowed
        to lose your earlobe-virginity.

The Ear-piercer disappoints at first glance,
        glasses on black braided string
around her neck. No Greco, she has
        the air of a seamstress, birdlike, dun
cast of female plumage in her dress.
        It's when she twists a small brass key
in an ornate but crusty lock, opens
        a pirate chest to lift an earring, finger
a little gold balloon that snaps off and on,
        clamped on top of seed pearls
and baguettes, explaining as she clips it
        with a snap: *These are coach covers
or carriage covers. They hid jewels from
        highwaymen who otherwise
would rip them off, tearing the earlobes,*
        pulling her own ear as she spoke,

– it's then you see through her disguise,
    her camouflage, see her as transformer,
like those who flash scissors and pins
    instead of wings, change things utterly
with cloth, zippers, buttons, hems.
    She wizards you with silver and turquoise,
your choice, drawn to the softer, malleable metal
    and the semi-precious, magpied
from some auction room, estate, bazaar.
    How come the galloping masked men
never figured out the gold balloons?
    But her bright bird-eyes keep you stum.
Besides, the Ear-piercer is busy punching
    through the vertebra that crunches
like a stapler in your ear. The stapler leaves
    gold studs in so the holes don't close.

The body thinks they're wounds, she says.
    Don't touch the gold studs for ten days.
The turquoise drops, your birthday present,
    go in the next day, deliver an infection
like a kind of faux VD, small price to pay
    for standing on the top rung of that ladder
slanting from your bedroom window for some time now,
    not Jacob's uphill route but
equally steep, its narrow splintery steps
    and icy spaces hit and miss in darkness
and daylight as you climb down, bit by bit,
    rear back up in a sweat of cowardice,
afraid but crazy to elope with someone waiting
    in The Village, in a studio, sipping
espresso as her earrings sway like Greco
    to low, fierce notes that echo in her throat.

Richard Lambert

Bees

A store of light, a shoal,
a smallness of sunlight-darkness,
pips, ghosts,
a slowness amongst the trees.

Ben Lerner

Dilation

I

We need to harness the vaguely erotic disappointment that attends
    the realization you aren't being followed,
keys gripped between the fingers, ready to strike at the eyes
The after-image of byzantine gold leaf dissolving in the trees when
    we emerge from the museum must be harnessed,
and the delicate carnation of the sky at the rooftop screening,
and the dress of the hostess, its exploration of formative drives

If you are anything like me, you emerge from the hospital's automatic
    doors into the heat and glare of its parking lot
unable to recall the colour of the rental or the demands of practical
    reason
You surface from the subway to find it's fully night and hard to
    remember the preceding generation's claims
for disjunction, you saw the child of a Turkish diplomat fall from a
    penthouse balcony,
curled up on a floor model at the SoHo Crate & Barrel when you
    received the terrible news

from a poem that probably dates from 1939, address to an adjacent
    posterity
Green eyeshadow and surprising gentleness of the saleswoman who
    asks if I'm OK must be harnessed if we
are to surpass camp and apathy, plain-clothes security closing in
You feel emancipated briefly from fragmentation when the D train
    emerges onto the Manhattan Bridge,
vertically polarized light entering the water, seventy-six storeys of
    rippled steel refusing to be actual

all at once, stand and offer your seat to an old man who isn't there,
    listen politely to his demand for a theatre
that combines distance and empathy, false proscenium lit to reveal
evaporating value, the delicate carnation that follows heat and glare

II

I came into the cities at a time in which the service industry employed
    a swift underclass of Spanish-speaking labourers
I came into the cities when the art world's post-medium pluralism
    valorized stupidity
In the midst of weather patterns of increasing extremity, I came into
    the cities, unsure if I should say *gracias* to the man
refilling my glass, notes of chlorine, antidepressants in trace amounts
One way was enumerating the bad forms of alienated collective
    power: breathing hot particles from Japan,

bundled debt, another way was passing beyond the reach of friends,
    to internalize an allegory,
tracking the dilation where aorta meets heart, minor tremor in the hand
Part of me wants to say there is a mock-oratorical mode capable of
    vitalizing critical agency and part of me
wants to praise the maple's winged samaras, the distance achieved
    from the parent tree,
but mainly I want to argue they're one thing, real if indefensible

like cities in time, spinning as they fall
My role in the slaughter doesn't disqualify the beauty I find in all
    forms of sheltered flame, little votive polis,
that I eat while others starve does not refute the promise of dimming
    house lights, weird fullness of the instant
before music, that I ventriloquize when I address you *is* the marker of
    my voice, important source
of syrup and tonewood, coming to you live

from the ellipses of compotier and vase, grave air of a masterpiece, its
    notes of ozone and exhaust,
jasmine in trace amounts, tracking the dilation of new forms
of private temporality into public architecture, glass curtains as they
    dim

III

The ideal is visible through its antithesis like small regions of warm
  blue underpainting and this is its late
July realization, I'm sorry, I know you were expecting more
I'm not going to lecture the neighbour kid with the hydrant key about
  conserving water for posterity
until I can think of a better idea for the spontaneous formation of
  a public, however brief
By the time you read this, if you are close enough to read this, if you
  are reading this

a threat to the first person was called in, prompting its evacuation,
  a panic you should take advantage of
in order to compose a face, test predicates against, walk to Sunset
  Park and watch the soft-winged kites
at magic hour when light appears immanent to the lit, warm blue
  scattering
in the gaps between buildings and print, you can feel the content
  streaming
The ideal is a kind of longitudinal subject in which the poem is a note
  saying where I left you keys

and a bottle of green wine, sea-rise visible in the compound eye,
  mosaic image, flicker effect
in which objects must move in order to persist, thus the preference of
  bees for windblown flowers,
thus the analogy collapses like a colony, prompting its evacuation,
  but the formal capacity for likening still shines
through its antithesis, feel it misfiring, vaguely erotic disappointment
  that combines
distance and empathy, carnation fading from the contrails, trying
  to conceive

in a ready-to-assemble bed as the metropole shifts East
I believe there is a form of apology both corporate and incantatory
  that could convene the future it begs for leniency,
inherited dream you can put anything in: antithetical blue, predicate
  green

Frances Leviston

Disinformation

I am making jelly
for my nephew's fourth birthday party,
any flavour as long as it's red,
bouncy cubes snipped and stirred into hot water
in a cloudy Pyrex dish,
rediscovering the secret of isinglass,
or is it horse gelatin, while a radio announcer
intimates that certain unpopular
facts about the operations
hitherto repressed, like signs removed
from crossroads and bridges in occupied lands,
can now be revealed, if we just stay tuned.

Party-bags designed
to please infants pile on the counter,
too-bright colours badly drawn, blue napkins,
party-poppers, my red hands
put cylinders of sausages on cocktail sticks
(these pass for traditions),
and all the time I listen to them talk
fluently about foreknowledge, proactivity, stations.
It is winter,
treacherous to walk.
The children are on their way by now,
adults too, bundled against the promise of snow,

and the entertainer, with tricks and jokes
hidden under a blanket in the boot of his Volvo,
limp balloons into which he will blow
his lungs full of ideal animals, practises misdirection.
I chop yellow cheese. Out the kitchen window
the whirligig turns; metal spokes
merciless as diagrams

cutting the air
no clothing softens, tiny gems
icing the nodes where their lines intersect.
Every extant leaf is fixed
with glitter where the glue's dried clear.

Pippa Little

Axis

Lying in his last bed
my father remembers his feet
far down in the dark, lost
like a ticket:

cold and soft untouchables
they are forgetting about shoes,
about the metallic lips of stairs,
the earth's axis.

Medbh McGuckian

BUTTERMILK SHADE

The earth beside you
is full of bulbs:
what, if anything, can be done?

Summer and winter meet on the trees.
Something seems gone from the garden
and you cannot tell what.

Large black umbrellas
had been hung from the ceiling
by way of decoration,

beings in the same place
yet not together –
the amusement of the dead

at our wanting to live on,
to buy rainforest, or cloudforest,
and leave it undisturbed

while the warmth from our fields
pours itself unrequited into space
and frightens the flowers blue.

A grey cloud in one piece
plaits dark on the sea
through the crimson pulp of sunset.

Daylight is almost powerless
in the room. For minutes of years
it addresses the fog

on this nocturnal side of speech.
And furniture talks also
in this way:

a taper lighting the stair-rods,
a bulb burning out in the porch
all night;

the vibration of that which is perfect,
the glow at its edges,
is watching the world change.

Christopher Meredith

The Record Keepers

> *One thousand one hundred and thirty was the age of*
> *Christ when there were four years in succession without*
> *there being any history…*
> — Brut y Tywysgyon/Chronicle of the Princes

That day, Brother Cynan in his magpie habit
stepped from the Scriptorium door.
Daniel and Owain paced by the pond
measured steps kicking at their gowns
and talked unheard.
Cynan threw crumbs to the sparrows,
rubbed his whiskery tonsure,
felt food easing through him, sighed
and looked back to the silent page.
    Rain fell then didn't.
The wheel of the sky
did its diurnal turn, its equinoctial tilt.
He slept and woke,
stared back at Taurus's red eye.
The masses passed.
    Was God asleep
or was this an awakening?
    One day in a ripening barley field
Cynan watched the quietness of butterflies,
white and many mazing and dipping
to blooms among the stalks.
They wrote the history of air.

                        *

Consider. The edited highlight could also be
the bit where the wicketkeeper yawns
rubbing an eyelash from his face.
Or think of Watts's minotaur –
he *could* be waiting on those battlements

for the freight of virgins, but maybe not,
that crushed bird no symbol, just a slip.
Perhaps there's no more narrative
than watching sky.

       *

Then, at the bottom of a sea
like a hell on a church wall
hagfish fattened on a rotting monster
blind jaws working.
Fished up, they oozed and rotted in the sun.
And then a monster with a crown
battened on bad meat and found it good,
till suddenly he stopped.
Some inconsequential picture
stayed on his dying retinas –
a cobweb in a corner, say,
as his brain shut down.
A courtier will have hesitated,
checked for breath, flicked at last
a finger at the still eye
(in the royal jelly the unseen image
of the cobweb shivers)
and hurried out.
So in the rigor mortis of a king
Process stiffened to event and story woke
and plot and consequence began again.

       *

Brother Cynan in his magpie habit
took his knife and opened the Scriptorium door.
Somewhere in him till he died would be
an unheard talk, some sparrows on a path
small scriptless books that eddied in still air.
   He said, *The thing about the ineffable is* –
and shrugged and pared the quill,
split the nib, and reached for ink.

David Morley

The lil to lel oprey the kekkeno mushe's puvior
and to keir the choveno foky mer of buklipen and shillipen,
is wusted abri the Raioriskey rokkaring ker.

'Your language, Gypsy,' mocks John Clare, 'is borrowed goods
or burglary. You smash up English to be hardly understood
then dispart under the drowk of your dark tongue's dossities.'
'And you?' smiles Wisdom, 'Folks say you dine on dictionaries
yet you remain a blank child, as foal-minded as any of my ponies –
tethered by a line, you still nose and slurp at flowers and clovers.'
But his friend is no longer listening to him: he dythers in miracles –
glimpt hedges are freshing with roosting starnels; a whirlipuff reels
as if something danced in it, and tazzles the grasses, ruffs the corn
where its wands are ramping, strows and stirtles the sprotes upon
the spirey blaze as the Gypsy progs it, forcing sparks with a stickle
to twinkle from the flaze. 'Gently now, brother,' urges the Gypsy,
'Warm your mind before you write of the things you see or hear.
They might not be of this world.' 'But my words are,' breathes Clare.

Helen Mort

STAINLESS STEPHEN

He haunts the chippies mostly,
nodding his approval
at the puns: *A Salt & Battery,*
In Cod We Trust.

He's dressed up to the nines
in stainless shoes, a plated vest,
two spoons for a bow tie. A fork
to comb his sleek, black hair.

He says: *I'm aimless comma*
brainless comma Stainless Stephen
semi-colon semi-conscious
ordering my chips full stop

And when the shop lads
shove him out into the cold,
he knows a pub across the river
where the doors will never shut,

a shell between the empty works,
where brambles twine around the pumps
and every glass is draped
with webs. Where men stride in

still sweating from the braziers
that vanished thirty years ago
and tug their collars,
loosening the noose of heat.

The jukebox hasn't changed its tune
since '71. The landlord stands,
a statue at the bar, as Stainless
saunters in and tips his silver hat,

surveys his audience –
the roughed-up chairs, the yawning
window panes, the shabby walls
that echo back each joke

as if they know them off by heart.
Semi-quaver, semi-frantic,
Stainless croons the golden oldies,
sing-alongs to sway to,

here in Sheffield
where they drink till dawn
and beg for encores, know
there's no such thing as *Time*.

Jean O'Brien

MERMAN

I had been working in the fish farm for weeks,
that one near the river outlet and the sea.
I didn't like the work we were constantly
wet, dirty, didn't like the men there either.
They were insolent, often dropped small fry
and crushed them underfoot. One in particular
Glaucus, tall, muscular cast his sea-green eyes over me,
tried to lure me as I tipped phosphorus feed
into the holding pens that smoked and stank
and made mist veils I tried to hide within.

One day he walked towards the tanks
waders held in his large hands, he was chewing
on a herb he said was magical, always urging
me to eat it. I would not bite. Anyway whatever way
it was, he leaned to pull the waders on, both legs
got caught in one boot and over he flipped.
I cast around for help, no-one was there. I went back.
He was emerging from amongst the shoals
of salmon, clinging to his single wader
up to his waist were the glittering scales of smolts.

He rose shaking, coloured sequins waterfalling
as he tried to right himself and beckoned me for help.
I took the bait and when I caught him,
we stumbled, he landed me and pinned me down,
I looked, held his eyes, it was early the rising sun
was flooding them with hooks of golden light. I said No.
He parted my thighs and when it was over,
untangled his legs, shook the silver armour
from himself, his eyes had lost their lustre.

I left distraught and walked all day stumbling
over ditches and hillocks, stopped now and then
to eat, following the river to its source.
At so many hundred feet I rested where the stream
welled from the earth, cooled my toes, kicked gravel
into little pools and felt the flow snagging
in the waters of my womb. I cried and screamed
and shook my fists at the sky, knew then this birthing
pool was to be my fate, tried to obliterate
his sea-green eyes, his face, his terrible merman tail.

Rebecca O'Connor

THE LAKES

The wet here can break a person's heart with sheer persistence.
Imagine one day your husband's beard smells of damp dog,
his long johns stink of pondweed, and you think nothing –
or very little – of it. Until, one day,
you wake to find him looking up at you with wet spaniel eyes.
That's what it's like – an endless incoming tide.
The trick is to give him plenty of exercise.

John Osborne

We Should Call a Man

The bonnet of our Punto
is propped open with a wooden spoon.
My face and shirt are smudged with oil,
bits of engine are scattered across the front lawn
like children's toys.
You stand on the doorstep
with your arms folded, and say:
"We need to get a man in."

In our shed is a Flymo edge trimmer,
a Black & Decker Jigsaw,
a Bosch cordless screwdriver
still in their boxes
lined up like *Star Wars* collectables;
because whenever something goes wrong
you shake your head and I know you're thinking
of the time I tried to fix the washing machine
and flooded the utility room.

And when I fixed the guttering
the ladder fell to the floor. I had to wait on the roof
until you came home.
So when something needs doing
you say "We need to get a man in."

The stubs in my chequebook
read: *Man*
Man
Man
Man

There's a man in our living room now
trying to install a wireless connection.
He has been in there for two hours.
I take him a cup of tea
and see: his head in his hands, instruction book
thrown to the floor. Suddenly
we are equals.

Edward Ragg

ANTHEM AT MORNING

How wonderful it would be
in this brightest of mornings

to walk in the clear light
not of possibility

but purpose and to sing
in that same clear light

of the purpose that
in all possibility is today.

Maurice Riordan

It happened on the cinder path between the playing field
and the graveyard one afternoon in October
when all the leaves of the aspen flipped over
and stayed, the way a skirt might blow up and hold
in a gust of wind – except there was no wind,
one of those days when the thud of a football
hangs in the deadened air. But there was no thud,
no sound from man or bird. So I'd swear if I'd looked
at my watch just then the digits would have stuck

if I could have looked, for it must've been a time
when time was snagged in its fluid escapement
and in that lull no one can enter the world,
or leave it; the cars stand on the motorway,
the greyhound's legs are knotted above the track,
a missile is framed in mid-flight, no sound
comes from the child's mouth, the open beak,
and the shoal of herring is a sculpted cloud
shimmering under the glass of the rolling downs.

At this moment, when the joker palms the room-key,
the punching fist can be opened, the egg slipped back
under the nesting bird, and each of us could scurry
to forestall one mischance, or undo one wrong choice
whose thorn of consequence has lodged till now,
before whatever it is keeps the world scary
and true breaks loose. A squirrel turns tail
overhead, a chestnut rolls to the ground, and with it
a drawn-out scream arrives from childhood.

IRISH

That gleam the sand has before the tide,
its fish-skin-wet and soft-cement texture,
so it stands out as if above the strand
– is there a word for it in Irish? So one
oarsman seeing its oily sheen shouts
Tarraingimís chuige! And the other nods.

In English, there's a word I've forgotten
for those reflections on the underside
of the prow... I see them, or their cognates,
when the early sun is on the pond
at home, and it sends bubbles of light
along the dusty mahogany sideboard.

No one I've ever asked knows the word.
And watching the bubbles now like cells
in a Petri dish, it's hard to think one pulse
of code sent brain to brain would bring to mind
their wisp-fire on the creosoted wood,
together with wind and sky this end of day,

the last before we pack our bags and up sticks
for London... already there's the petite mort
of items missed or chucked, as the boat heads
for port, the rowers pulling crosswind hard
into the swell, and I feel the earth's slow spin
and seasonal lurch in the slight ocean chill.

Yet the word is there in Melville, or Conrad,
where I might still read it; snagged, too, up
some old boreen of memory on a dozen
rusty neurons, from where it could slip loose,
or I'll overhear it spoken on the pier,
or happen on the right philologist.

And then, as the tongue recoups the sound
effortlessly, the word will shed its lure
and be an all-too-easy hook for this effect
of light hitting the sliding planes of water
(which for me also involves my armchair,
the screen, solitude, the grip of coffee).

I'll find there was a gain to the small disablement,
and long for dreams in which I've spoken Irish,
or once Norwegian – no words as such…
just a moist pleasurable chemical blaze
of utterance, not unlike that queer looming
of the strand, where the tide has yet to reach.

Roger Robinson

TRINIDAD GOTHIC

Some of the women in Point Ligoure had already been arrested
for seasoning their husbands' food with a pinch of cement powder.
A stone grew. Grit in an oyster. Chalk in a rooster's gizzard.
Within two weeks they lay dead with a wolf's stone in their stomachs.

The women all had a good reason for this mode of murder
and passed the method on to other women with the same cause.
But alas, too many men of Point Ligoure died at once,
which prompted an investigation, which led to a mass autopsy,

and flaps of stomachs peeled back to find stone after stone,
which led to aunties, grandmothers and girlfriends being led
away in daydresses and handcuffs as other women looked on.
But one clever woman in Point Ligoure found a new way.

You leave an iron out overnight, then before sunrise
you pummel the base of that iron into the soles
of his feet, and you cause an instant untraceable heart attack.
At Point Ligoure, you'll see a dozen irons glinting in the moonlight.

Martin Rowson

ANDREW MARVELL

Metaphysicist ANDREW MARVELL
Put down his quill sighing, 'Oh swell!
      Where's my one chance of joy
      When my mistress is coy?
What are we to do? Oh, 'Kin 'ell!

Had we but world enough, plus the time,
This coyness, lady, were no crime,
      But what's the point if
      We wait 'til we're both stiff?
'Cos the dead, luv, are well past their prime!

But at my back I always hear
Time's wing'd chariot hurrying near;
      Deserts of vast eternity
      Will scupper paternity
If we don't make haste right now, m'dear!

So come on, babe, take off that sweater!
If you like I can use this French letter
      'Fore I discharge my load!'
      (Though in MARVELL's own ode
I concede the last stanza reads better…)

John W Sexton

In and Out of Their Heads

After he had proved irrefutably
that angels don't live on the heads of pins
or in the green cities of verdigris
that he scraped from the mute faces of coins,

Professor Lightshade discovered yeast-men,
frothing in the head with the minds of gods,
inhabiting the flat circular pen
commonly known as a ladybird's spot.

Inebriated for eternity,
smashed on fumes from their own fermenting brains,
ferried from bush to bush and tree to tree,
drunken passengers of the insect trains

the yeast-men exist devoid of futures,
travel no further than their own stupors.

Catherine Smith

My cat bites a sparrow's neck,
                drops it on the cream wool rug;
chomps contentedly through
                its grape-dark heart and pink lungs.
He leaves its neat head – both
                oil-black eyes; two tail feathers,
a bright red smear, then pads away.
                As I stand at the sink, scrubbing
bloodstains, I tell myself he's just
                obeying instincts – a sparrow
is prey to him; he cannot know
                in ancient China it was linked
to the penis, sometimes eaten
                for its potency, or in Greek myth,
an attribute of Aphrodite; or that
                in Western Art, a woman
holding a sparrow is a wanton.
                But as the water pinks, my eyes
sting with tears, because
                this creature was beautiful
and innocent and now it is dead.
                I think of Lesbia's pet sparrow,
limp in her lap; how she wept
                and wept until her eyes were raw.

Jean Sprackland

MOVING THE PIANO

It was damp in its joints, hamstrung and hipshot.
It still had a grubby mouthful of elephant.
The casewood hankered
after the big trees of the empire.

It was all stubborn resistance,
groaning and slubbering, innards jangling.
Something broke loose with a clunk.
We balanced the lid on its weak hinges

but the thing had slipped deep
into the interstitial dark.
The frame looked quaint as a spinning jenny.
It stank of old felt and lamentations.

It would take two strong men
and a third to watch the doorposts.
It would take a dolly, a humpstrap and two blankets.
There would be cursing at the turn of the stairs

and it would be a dead weight, passive as an invalid,
knowing its time has gone, but wanting only
to be left alone in its own home,
in its own wavering patch of light

while the clamorous room fades
to a tinnitus of dust and dead wasps.

Anne Stevenson

The ancient belief that body lets go its ghost
Only at death, like invisible thistledown – no!
I'd sooner believe the opposite is so,
That flesh is the flyaway guest a spacious host
Breathes in and out, an element at most
That in transmission clings and starts to grow,
Nameless today, tomorrow a face, a show,
Parented, schooled, determinedly self-engrossed,
Till eyes' exchanges seem reliable,
And 'Here I am!' agrees with 'We have seen.'
A few, though, slip behind the human screen,
Where what they meet's so wonder-terrible
They never dare pretend again they've been
More than a voice in the void, a link between.

Matthew Sweeney

Ghost

A man egged another on to kill him,
then appeared as a vengeful ghost,
whispering to his killer that the cost
of his enjoyment of that final whim
would be nothing less than suicide.
No lifetime spent in prison's care,
not even a blast of the electric chair
would do. He'd need to have died
by the same hand as the other man,
on the same day, in the same place,
and if the killer should prefer to run,
the ghost would float before his face,
hissing that he was no one, no one,
and he would never win this race.

George Szirtes

ACTUALLY, YES

Somewhere between the highly spectacular *No*
and the modest *yes* of the creatures, word
arises and claims its space. *No* can afford
fireworks and a grand entrance, but *yes* must go
barefoot across floorboards. *No* can extend
its franchise over the glossolalia
of the imagination: *yes* discovers failure
in a preposition impossible to offend.
No demands success and receives reviews
of the utmost luminosity while *yes*
is damned with faint praise. *No* profits by excess:
yes has little to say and even less to lose.
The full Shakespearean ending is *No* with its raised brow.
Yes disappears off stage and will not take a bow.

Look, here's a very small *yes*. Now watch it run
its almost invisible race through nature. How
does it know where to go? Where is it now?
Right there! Just there! Like a picture of no one
in particular it looks surprised to be seeing
itself approach a selfhood hardly likely. See
it hesitate as it approaches the sheer possibility
of emergence on the very edge of being.
Always off-centre, its marginal affirmation
of life's distant provinces will be rewarded
with the briefest of smiles when smiles can be afforded
while monstrous *No* boldly addresses the nation.
But now and then, the honest citizen will confess,
when asked, to a weakness of sorts, whispering *Yes*.

Well, *yes*. Actually, *yes*.

Claire Trévien

THE SHIPWRECKED HOUSE II

After Frank O'Hara

When waves were far enough away
and the pumpkin seeds still as amber
in the treasure chest, the calls tumblingly
came to crook the paintings, writings, all.

Now your voice falls like a coin to the ocean's floor
and the house is dragged apart by the fractures
of your smiles – the thought of its absence echoes
unbelievably – our breath opens like a stiff drawer.

You are everywhere and nowhere, you are
the unfinished cup of tea and its straw,
dipped like a paintbrush. I want to keep
the yoghurts that went out of date yesterday.

Lucy Anne Watt

THE TREE POSITION

My son went to war in a country the colour of sand. And came back
in a light beech box hefted on the shoulders of six strong men.

And this and my son turned me into a tree.
All the leaves of my happiness fell from me.

I hooked my fingers into the sky and my roots embraced
the last of my son. Earth to earth as they say.

But ash is the taste in my mouth. Ash, the colour of my sky and skin;
of the remains of my love. In parturition I did not scream.

I bit down hard on a towel, a rag, so as better to hear
my boy's first shout. As I embody his last that I never heard.

And I watched the Prime Minister pass. The young PM
aka Warlord, aka Sancho Panza to another's Quixote,

aka Pinball Player with the lives of young men. And I saw in him
        an actor.
An actor can act big while being a fool.

And even with my fingers in the sky, and my roots in cinders,
and rain always in my eyes, strung between

the hell of my love and the heaven of release,
suspended in the perpetual winter

of barrenness reprised,
the PM looked right through me. And I decided

Only lawyers think that wars are arguments to be won. But wars are
     always lost.
In the heart. In the home. In the wheelchair. In the widow's tiny
     portion.

In the fatherless child. In mothers
like me. In the compound nature of the cost.

Soldiers obey orders. But where were mine?
When did I contract to be as I now am?

So I cursed the PM. I will not say how. I was one
grieving tree. But the war goes on. I am a forest now.

CK Williams

WRITERS WRITING DYING

Many I could name but won't who'd have been furious to die while
    they were sleeping but did –
outrageous, they'd have lamented, and never forgiven the death
    they'd construed for themselves
being stolen from them so rudely, so crudely, without feeling
    themselves like rubber gloves
stickily stripped from the innermostness they'd contrived to hoard
    for so long – all of it gone,
squandered, wasted, on what? *Death*, crashingly boring as long as
    you're able to think and write it.

Think, write, write, think: just keep galloping faster and you won't
    even notice you're dead.
The hard thing's when you're not thinking or writing and as far as
    you know you are dead
or might as well be, with no word for yourself, just that suction-
    shush like a heart pump or straw
in a milk shake and death which once wanted only to be sung back
    to sleep with its tired old fangs
has me in its mouth! – and where the hell are you that chunk of
    dying we used to call Muse?

Well, dead or not, at least there was that dream, of some scribbler,
    some think-and-write person,
maybe it was yourself, soaring in the sidereal void, and not only
    that, you were holding a banjo
and gleefully strumming, and singing, jaw swung a bit under and
    off to the side the way crazily
happily people will do it – singing songs or not even songs, just
    lolly-molly syllable sounds
and you'd escaped even from language, from having to gab, from
    having to write down the idiot gab.

But in the meantime isn't this what it is to be dead, with that
   Emily-fly buzzing over your snout
that you're singing almost as she did; so what matter if you died
   in your sleep or rushed towards dying
like the Sylvia-Hart part of the tribe who ceased too quickly to be
   and left out some stanzas?
You're still aloft with your banjoless banjo, and if you're dead or
   asleep who really cares?
Such fun to wake up though! Such fun too if you don't! Keep
   dying! Keep writing it down!

Shortlisted Writers

Best Collection

REBECCA GOSS grew up in Suffolk and recently returned there after living for 20 years in Liverpool, a city she loves. At the age of 15, she won the WH Smith Young Writers' Award, judged that year by Ted Hughes. *Her Birth* is an autobiographical sequence about her daughter, Ella, who was born with an incurable heart condition and lived for only 16 months. 'I worried that this subject would be too sad for the reader. I started out censoring the poems a little but soon realised I had to tell it exactly how it happened. I want to talk about her – I miss her – and the poems let me do that but in a very controlled way.' Her biggest influence is the American author Jayne Anne Phillips and she describes herself as a 'frustrated short story writer'.

GLYN MAXWELL was born in Welwyn Garden City, a town he describes as 'one man's dream of how daily life could be better'. He studied at Oxford before moving to America to work with Derek Walcott. He cites WH Auden as an influence along with Louis MacNeice, Robert Frost and Edward Thomas. *Pluto* looks at the before-and-after of love and the underworld of internet dating. It is, he says, his most personal collection yet. He has written plays, operas, films and novels as well as poetry and is currently working on a collection of poems which 'leaf through the shit in the newspapers and try to make songs out of it'.

SINÉAD MORRISSEY has lived in Germany, Japan and New Zealand. She says she is 'drawn to historical subjects, and to issues concerning looking and sight'. *Parallax*, her fifth collection, examines what is caught and lost in the time-freezing act of photography. A parallax is the difference in the apparent position of an object when seen from two different points, and applies particularly to astronomy and photography. She lectures in creative writing at Queen's University, Belfast.

JACOB POLLEY was artist-in-residence for three months at his local newspaper where he wrote a poem a day. He has published a novel, *Talk of the Town*, written in a phonetic version of Cumbrian dialect. *The Havocs*, his third volume of poetry, conjures horror and unsettling comedy from traditional forms and makes the ordinary seem strange. On being asked what a prize nomination meant to him he said, 'there's no bigger thrill than imagining the book I've written in a stranger's hands.' He teaches at the University of St Andrews.

MICHAEL SYMMONS ROBERTS became a journalist on graduating from Oxford. He writes for radio, makes documentary films and collaborates with composers. He chose the title for his fifth collection of poetry, 'in response to the old high street traders called drysalters, who were dealers in gums, drugs, poisons and powders.' The word is also 'a nod to the psalter, those medieval day-books that contained psalms, but also jokes and cartoons and marginalia'. He admires John Donne, Elizabeth Bishop, Marianne Moore and John Berryman. Every poem in *Drysalter* is 15 lines long: the next challenge, he says, will be 'to force myself to write a poem with a sixteenth line'.

Best First Collection

EMILY BERRY grew up in London, the child of two writers. At school, a teacher played her a recording of John Berryman reading his *Dream Songs*, which she calls 'a formative poetry experience'. She says, 'I like humour in a poem, but also agony. *Dream Songs* are definitely a touchstone for me.' *Dear Boy*, her first collection of poetry, took her about seven years to write.

MARIANNE BURTON recited poetry from early childhood, because her mother wanted her daughters to 'speak proper'. She won her first poetry prize for an elegy to a dead butterfly. She qualified as a solicitor, working in the City advising Friendly Societies and as a director on the board of a pharmaceutical company. Both jobs have fuelled her writing: 'People wanted me to understand the intricacies of their lives.' In 2010, she was tutored at Ty Newydd by Gillian Clarke and Carol Ann Duffy, who encouraged her to put together her first collection, *She Inserts the Key*.

STEVE ELY started writing poetry on his seventeenth birthday. A former Sunday League footballer, revolutionary socialist and secondary school head teacher, he lives in the West Riding of Yorkshire and is fascinated by the history of England and the English propensity for violence. In *Oswald's Book of Hours*, he sets up the seventh-century King of Northumbria as an alternative patron saint of England and writes a 'handbook of devotions' loosely modelled on a medieval book of hours. His other works include a novel and five unpublished poetry collections.

HANNAH LOWE was born in Ilford to an English mother and Jamaican-Chinese father. She began writing poems aged 29 after her father, a professional gambler, died of cancer and her mother had a stroke. She cites Gerard Manley Hopkins, Anne Sexton and Mark Doty as influences. 'I had been suppressing a lot of grief over a sustained period of time and poetry opened a door on that pain. I found that I could revisit the past in my poems, and contain it, or alter it even.' *Chick*, her first collection, stems from an Arvon course in 2010 in which the Scottish poet John Glenday suggested she write about her father.

DAN O'BRIEN is an American playwright and poet living in Los Angeles. He was raised near New York City and describes his family as working-class Irish-American. He started writing poetry at school, inspired by Anne Sexton, and won a scholarship to Brown University. In 2007, he heard Pulitzer Prize-winning war reporter Paul Watson speak of being haunted by a soldier he had photographed in 1993 in Mogadishu. After meeting Watson, O'Brien turned their exchanges into the poems in *War Reporter*. They have also collaborated on a play and an opera.

ADAM WHITE was born in Dublin in 1978. He grew up in Youghal, in County Cork. He worked for years as a carpenter/joiner in Ireland and in France before studying English and French at the National University of Ireland in Galway. It was here that he began writing poetry and reciting it at the North Beach Poetry Nights slams in Galway's Crane Bar. *Accurate Measurements* grew out of a poem composed for the slams in April 2009. The other poems in the book were written in Galway, Cork, the city of Angers in France and most recently rural Normandy, where he now works in a secondary school.

Best Single Poem

PATIENCE AGBABI was born in London in 1965, to Nigerian parents. She has been poet-in-residence at both a tattoo parlour and Eton College. She is a popular performer, influenced by dub poetry and rap, and her work has been broadcast, appeared on the London Underground and etched into human skin. She is currently a Fellow in Creative Writing at Oxford Brookes University. Her new collection will be published by Canongate in 2014.

CJ ALLEN came to poetry via Ken Dodd, whose radio shows taught him, he says, 'about the power of language harnessed to a keen sense of rhythm and timing'. He achieved '45 glorious seconds of radio fame' when he wrote and sold a commercial radio jingle for Morrison's supermarkets in 1976. One of his poems is engraved on a granite rock in the Derbyshire Peaks, others have appeared in *Poetry Review* and *Modern Painters*. 'Form,' he says, 'is central to my work.' He reads and re-reads the poetry of John Ashbery and John Schuyler.

NICK MACKINNON worked as a psychogeriatric nurse in the early 1980s before teaching maths and English at Winchester College: both experiences inform his writing. He won the £5,000 Hippocrates prize (NHS section) for a poem imagining the changing role of a psychiatric hospital from the point of view of a local landmark. He spent his teenage years in Ardrishaig on the long finger of land that points to Ireland.

ROSIE SHEPPERD worked in banking and financial journalism in London and New York until 2004, when she discovered a talent for poetry. She finds food inspiring: 'There's a deliberation in my enjoyment of tastes which is very similar to my enjoyment of words and images.' She experiments with the syntax of spoken speech: pauses, emphases, the rises and falls of verbal expression. Poets she admires include Paul Muldoon, Paul Durcan, Elizabeth Bishop and Robert Lowell, and she 'never stops reading' Raymond Carver.

HUGO WILLIAMS, born in 1942, is the son of the actor Hugh Williams and the model and actress Margaret Vyner-Williams: he has portrayed his father in his poetry as handsome, masterful and remote, 'a stiff theatrical man'. He has said the 'real background story' of his 1970s was 'a record-breaking dole-run', though by the time he won the 2000 TS Eliot Prize for *Billy's Rain* he had clearly established himself in the top ranks of his poetry generation. His work is characterised by candour, irony and brio – even when writing about the dialysis treatment which currently keeps him from contributing as frequently as readers would like to the *Times Literary Supplement*.

Publisher acknowledgements

Dannie Abse · CATS · *Speak, Old Parrot* · Hutchinson

Patience Agbabi · THE DOLL'S HOUSE · Poetry Reveiw

CJ Allen · EXPLAINING THE PLOT OF 'BLADE RUNNER' TO MY MOTHER
WHO HAS ALZHEIMER'S · Troubadour International Poetry Prize

Simon Armitage · POUNDLAND · Stand Magazine

Paul Batchelor · BROTHER COAL · Times Literary Supplement

Kaddy Benyon · ICE FISHING · *Milk Fever* · Salt

Tara Bergin · AT THE GARAGE · STAG-BOY · *This is Yarrow* · Carcanet

Emily Berry · Two BUDGIES · THE INTERNATIONAL YEAR OF THE POEM ·
Dear Boy · Faber and Faber

Marianne Burton · FIELDFARE · THE ANAGRAM KID · *She Inserts the Key* ·
Seren

Gillian Clarke · WHO KILLED THE SWAN? · Agenda Poetry Journal

Jennifer Copley · FIRST WINTER WITHOUT THE DOG · Dream Catcher

Nichola Deane · YESTERDAY'S CHILD · The Rialto

Patricia Debney · WHITSTABLE SPIT · *Littoral* · Shearsman Books

Oliver Dixon · AT LLANTWITT BEACH · *Human Form* · Penned in
the Margins

Andrew Elliott · SCHOLARSHIP BOY *from* THE MAN'S MIDDLE LEG IS A
LADY'S LEG · *Mortality Rate* · CB Editions

Steve Ely · INCIPIT EUANGELIUM SECUNDUM WAT TYLER · COMPLINE:
CORONATION OF THE VIRGIN · *Oswald's Book of Hours* · Smokestack Books

Matthew Francis · FROM LONDON TO ARCHANGEL *from* MUSCOVY ·
PHONEBOX ELEGY · *Muscovy* · Faber and Faber

Rebecca Goss · TOAST · STRETCH MARKS · *Her Birth* ·
Carcanet/Northern House

Marilyn Hacker · THE STRANGER'S MIRROR · PN Review

Mark Halliday · LOIS IN THE SUNNY TREE · CLASSIC BLUNDER ·
Thresherphobe · The University of Chicago Press

Robert Hampson · HOMELAND SECURITY · *Reworked Disasters* · Knives
Forks and Spoons Press

Jo Hemmant · AN ENGINE ROOM OFF THE COAST OF NORTH AFRICA ·
The Light Knows Tricks · Doire Press

Kirsten Irving · RECIPE FOR A SAINT · *Never Never Never Come Back* · Salt

Christopher James · THE PUB SIGN GIANT · *England Underwater* ·
Templar Poetry

Clive James · HOLDING COURT · Times Literary Supplement

Hilary Jupp · OUTING 1964 · Poetry News

Luke Kennard · THE FLAT BATTERY OF FLATTERY · *A Lost Expression* · Salt

Aileen La Tourette · THE EAR PIERCER · The Journal

Richard Lambert · BEES · *Night Journey* · Eyewear Publishing

Ben Lerner · DILATION · Granta Magazine

Frances Leviston · DISINFORMATION · Times Literary Supplement

Pippa Little · AXIS · *Overwintering* · Carcanet Oxford Poets

Hannah Lowe · FIVE WAYS TO LOAD A DICE · DANCE CLASS · *Chick* ·
Bloodaxe Books

Nick MacKinnon · THE METRIC SYSTEM · The Warwick Review

Glyn Maxwell · THE BYELAWS · THE WINDOW · *Pluto* · Picador Poetry

Medbh McGuckian · BUTTERMILK SHADE · *The High Caul Cap* ·
The Gallery Press

Christopher Meredith · THE RECORD KEEPERS · *Air Histories* · Seren

David Morley · ENGLISH · *The Gypsy and the Poet* · Carcanet

Sinéad Morrissey · THE COAL JETTY · THE MUTOSCOPE · *Parallax* · Carcanet

Helen Mort · STAINLESS STEPHEN · *Division Street* · Chatto & Windus

Dan O'Brien · THE WAR REPORTER PAUL WATSON ON CENSORSHIP ·
THE WAR REPORTER PAUL WATSON ON THE BOMBING OF THE DEAD ·
War Reporter · CB Editions

Jean O'Brien · MERMAN · *Merman* · Salmon Poetry

Rebecca O'Connor · THE LAKES · *We'll Sing Blackbird* · The Moth

John Osborne · WE SHOULD CALL A MAN · *Most People Aren't That Happy
Anyway* · Nasty Little Press

Jacob Polley · MANIFESTO FOR THE MAKESHIFT · SPIKE · *The Havocs* ·
Picador Poetry

Edward Ragg · ANTHEM AT MORNING · *A Force That Takes* ·
Cinnamon Press

Maurice Riordan · THE LULL · IRISH · *The Water Stealer* · Faber and Faber

Michael Symmons Roberts · FOOTFALL · THE VOWS · *Drysalter* · Cape Poetry

Roger Robinson · TRINIDAD GOTHIC · *The Butterfly Hotel* · Peepal Tree Press

Martin Rowson · ANDREW MARVELL · *The Limerickiad Vol. II* ·
Smokestack Books

John W Sexton · IN AND OUT OF THEIR HEADS · *The Offspring of the Moon* ·
  Salmon Poetry
Rosie Shepperd · A SEEDY NARRATIVE OR MOMENTS OF LYRICAL STILLNESS? ·
  Smith/Doorstop
Catherine Smith · SPARROWS · *Otherwhere* · Smith/Doorstop
Jean Sprackland · MOVING THE PIANO · *Sleeping Keys* · Cape Poetry
Anne Stevenson · THE VOICE · *Astonishment* · Bloodaxe Books
Matthew Sweeney · GHOST · *Horse Music* · Bloodaxe Books
George Szirtes · ACTUALLY, YES · *Bad Machine* · Bloodaxe Books
Claire Trévien · SHIPWRECKED HOUSE II · *The Shipwrecked House* ·
  Penned in the Margins
Lucy Anne Watt · THE TREE POSITION · Torbay Open Poetry Competition
Adam White · ROOFING · IN SHEFFIELD · *Accurate Measurements* ·
  Doire Press
CK Williams · WRITERS WRITING DYING · *Writers Writing Dying* ·
  Bloodaxe Books
Hugo Williams · FROM THE DIALYSIS WARD · London Review of Books

Previous winners of the Forward Prizes

BEST COLLECTION: Jorie Graham *PLACE* (Carcanet) 2012, John Burnside *Black Cat Bone* (Jonathan Cape) 2011, Seamus Heaney *Human Chain* (Faber and Faber) 2010, Don Paterson *Rain* (Faber and Faber) 2009, Mick Imlah *The Lost Leader* (Faber and Faber) 2008, Sean O'Brien *The Drowned Book* (Picador) 2007, Robin Robertson *Swithering* (Jonathan Cape) 2006, David Harsent *Legion* (Faber and Faber) 2005, Kathleen Jamie *The Tree House* (Picador) 2004, Ciaran Carson *Breaking News* (Gallery Press) 2003, Peter Porter *Max is Missing* (Picador) 2002, Sean O'Brien *Downriver* (Picador) 2001, Michael Donaghy *Conjure* (Picador) 2000, Jo Shapcott *My Life Asleep* (OUP) 1999, Ted Hughes *Birthday Letters* (Faber and Faber) 1998, Jamie McKendrick *The Marble Fly* (OUP) 1997, John Fuller *Stones and Fires* (Chatto) 1996, Sean O'Brien *Ghost Train* (OUP) 1995, Alan Jenkins *Harm* (Chatto) 1994, Carol Ann Duffy *Mean Time* (Anvil Press) 1993 and Thom Gunn *The Man with Night Sweats* (Faber and Faber) 1992

BEST FIRST COLLECTION: Sam Riviere *81 Austerities* (Faber and Faber) 2012, Rachael Boast *Sidereal* (Picador) 2011, Hilary Menos *Berg* (Seren) 2010, Emma Jones *The Striped World* (Faber and Faber) 2009, Kathryn Simmons *Sunday at the Skin Launderette* (Seren) 2008, Daljit Nagra *Look We Have Coming to Dover* (Faber and Faber) 2007, Tishani Doshi *Countries of the Body* (Aark Arts) 2006, Helen Farish *Intimates* (Jonathan Cape) 2005, Leontia Flynn *These Days* (Jonathan Cape) 2004, AB Jackson *Fire Stations* (Anvil Press) 2003, Tom French *Touching the Bones* (Gallery Press) 2002, John Stammers *Panoramic Lounge-bar* (Picador) 2001, Andrew Waterhouse *In* (The Rialto) 2000, Nick Drake *The Man in the White Suit* (Bloodaxe) 1999, Paul Farley *The Boy from the Chemist is Here to See You* (Picador) 1998, Robin Robertson *A Painted Field* (Picador) 1997, Kate Clanchy *Slattern* (Chatto) 1996, Jane Duran *Breathe Now, Breathe* (Enitharmon) 1995, Kwame Dawes *Progeny of Air* (Peepal Tree) 1994, Don Paterson *Nil Nil* (Faber and Faber) 1993 and Simon Armitage *Kid* (Faber and Faber) 1992

BEST SINGLE POEM: Denise Riley 'A Part Song' (London Review of Books) 2012, RF Langley 'To A Nightingale' (London Review of Books)

2011, Julia Copus 'An Easy Passage' (Magma) 2010, Robin Robertson 'At Roane Head' (London Review of Books) 2009, Don Paterson 'Love Poem for Natalie "Tusja" Beridze' (Poetry Review) 2008, Alice Oswald 'Dunt' (Poetry London) 2007, Sean O'Brien 'Fantasia on a Theme of James Wright' (Poetry Review) 2006, Paul Farley 'Liverpool Disappears for a Billionth of a Second' (The North) 2005, Daljit Nagra 'Look We Have Coming to Dover' (Poetry Review) 2004, Robert Minhinnick 'The Fox in the Museum of Wales' (Poetry London) 2003, Medbh McGuckian 'She is in the Past, She Has This Grace' (The Shop) 2002, Ian Duhig 'The Lammas Hireling' (National Poetry Competition) 2001, Tessa Biddington 'The Death of Descartes' (The Bridport Prize) 2000, Robert Minhinnick 'Twenty-five Laments for Iraq' (PN Review) 1999, Sheenagh Pugh 'Envying Owen Beattie' (New Welsh Review) 1998, Lavinia Greenlaw 'A World Where News Travelled Slowly' (Times Literary Supplement) 1997, Kathleen Jamie 'The Graduates' (Times Literary Supplement) 1996, Jenny Joseph 'In Honour of Love' (The Rialto) 1995, Iain Crichton Smith 'Autumn' (PN Review) 1994, Vicki Feaver 'Judith' (Independent on Sunday) 1993 and Jackie Kay 'Black Bottom' (Bloodaxe) 1992

If you would like to know more about the past, present or future of the Forward Prizes for Poetry or become involved with National Poetry Day, please register on our website www.forwardartsfoundation.org